Ithaca College
Ithaca, New York

Written by Sarah Hofius
Edited by Jim Seaman, James Balzer

*Additional contributions by Adam Burns, Omid Gohari,
Christina Koshzow, Chris Mason, Joey Rahimi,
Jon Skindzier, Luke Skurman, Tim Williams
and Kristen Burns*

ISBN # 1-59658-068-2
ISSN # 1551-101x
© Copyright 2005 College Prowler
All Rights Reserved
Printed in the U.S.A.
www.collegeprowler.com

Special thanks to Babs Carryer, Andy Hannah, LaunchCyte, Tim O'Brien, Bob Sehlinger, Thomas Emerson, Andrew Skurman, Barbara Skurman, Bert Mann, Dave Lehman, Daniel Fayock, Chris Babyak,The Donald H. Jones Center for Entrepreneurship, Terry Slease, Jerry McGinnis, Bill Ecenberger, Idie McGinty, Kyle Russell, Jacque Zaremba, Larry Winderbaum, Paul Kelly, Roland Allen, Jon Reider, Team Evankovich, Julie Fenstermaker, Lauren Varacalli, Abu Noaman, Jason Putorti, Mark Exler, Daniel Steinmeyer, Jared Cohon, Gabriela Oates, Tri Ad Litho, David Koegler, and Glen Meakem.

Bounce Back Team: Michelle Meredith, Anne Walters, and Channon Lucas

College Prowler™
5001 Baum Blvd.
Suite 456
Pittsburgh, PA 15213

Phone: (412) 697-1390, 1(800) 229-4675
Fax: (412) 697-1396, 1(800) 772-4972
E-mail: info@collegeprowler.com
Website: www.collegeprowler.com

Welcome to College Prowler™

During the writing of College Prowler's guidebooks, we felt it was critical that our content was unbiased and unaffiliated with any college or university. We think it's important that our readers get honest information and a realistic impression of the student opinions on any campus — that's why if any aspect of a particular school is terrible, we (unlike a campus brochure) intend to publish it. While we do keep an eye out for the occasional extremist — the cheerleader or the cynic — we take pride in letting the students tell it like it is. We strive to create a book that's as representative as possible of each particular campus. Our books cover both the good and the bad, and whether the survey responses point to recurring trends or a variation in opinion, these sentiments are directly and proportionally expressed through our guides.

College Prowler guidebooks are in the hands of students throughout the entire process of their creation. Because you can't make student-written guides without the students, we have students at each campus who help write, randomly survey their peers, edit, layout, and perform accuracy checks on every book that we publish. From the very beginning, student writers gather the most up-to-date stats, facts, and inside information on their colleges. They fill each section with student quotes and summarize the findings in editorial reviews. In addition, each school receives a collection of letter grades (A through F) that reflect student opinion and help to represent contentment, prominence, or satisfaction for each of our 20 specific categories. Just as in grade school, the higher the mark the more content, more prominent, or more satisfied the students are with the particular category.

Once a book is written, additional students serve as editors and check for accuracy even more extensively. Our bounce-back team — a group of randomly selected students who have no involvement with the project — are asked to read over the material in order to help ensure that the book accurately expresses every aspect of the university and its students. This same process is applied to the 200-plus schools College Prowler currently covers. Each book is the result of endless student contributions, hundreds of pages of research and writing, and countless hours of hard work. All of this has led to the creation of a student information network that stretches across the nation to every school that we cover. It's no easy accomplishment, but it's the reason that our guides are such a great resource.

When reading our books and looking at our grades, keep in mind that every college is different and that the students who make up each school are not uniform — as a result, it is important to assess schools on a case-by-case basis. Because it's impossible to summarize an entire school with a single number or description, each book provides a dialogue, not a decision, that's made up of 20 different topics and hundreds of student quotes. In the end, we hope that this guide will serve as a valuable tool in your college selection process. Enjoy!

OMID GOHARI ◯ CHRISTINA KOSHZOW ◯ CHRIS MASON ◯ JOEY RAHIMI ◯ LUKE SKURMAN ◯
Founders of College Prowler™

Table of Contents

Introduction from the Author

When I say that I'm a student at Ithaca College, I get one of three responses: the first is a blank stare, the second response is a brief word of congratulations, and the third is the inevitable question as to whether I go to the school where the movie "Road Trip" was filmed. Unfortunately for the questioners, it was Ithaca University in the movie, not Ithaca College. It is said, however, that there is some tie between the producers of the film and IC. Some people are disappointed to learn that I don't go to the school where Tom Green was depicted as one of the college tour guides, but others breathe a sigh of relief and tell me that I'm lucky to go to a school where things that happened on "Road Trip" don't actually occur, or at least not that often. Now that all possible confusion has been dealt with, it's time to move onto the real IC.

As you approach campus, it's hard not to be engulfed in the beauty of Ithaca, New York. The waterfalls, gorges, and ravines plus Lake Cayuga, the largest of New York's Finger Lakes, give the area a natural and clean feel. Sitting beside Cornell University, and housing one of the best college towns in the country, Ithaca, NY is lucky to have an atmosphere that simply can't be matched.

In the middle of all the surrounding beauty of Ithaca is IC, a private institution that is growing in leaps and bounds, earning more respect with every passing day. With IC's comprehensive education, students obtain a liberal arts education while receiving professional preparation. IC prides itself on its student-centered approach that emphasizes close interaction between students and faculty. Through education within IC's five different schools, as well as countless opportunities to get involved outside the classroom, students at IC take what they learn out into the real world. Each year the college sees an increase an applicants, and the word about IC's overall education is spreading.

Choosing where to spend four of the most important years of my life was one of the hardest decisions I've had to make. Looking back, I'm positive that I made the right choice. Whether this book steers you away from IC or reinforces your plans to enroll, I hope that reading the following facts and opinions will let you get a clear picture of IC, and will help you in your college-choosing decision.

Sarah Hofius, Author
Ithaca College

By the Numbers

General Information

Ithaca College
953 Danby Road
Ithaca, NY 14850

Control:
Private

Academic Calendar:
Semester

Religious Affiliation:
None

Founded:
1892

Website:
http://www.ithaca.edu

Main Phone:
(607) 274-3011

Admissions Phone:
(800) 429-4274

Student Body

Full-Time Undergraduates:
6,113

Part-Time Undergraduates:
147

**Full-Time Male
Undergraduates:**
2,635

**Full-Time Female
Undergraduates:**
3,478

Admissions

Overall Acceptance Rate:
57%

Early Decision Acceptance Rate:
50%

Regular Acceptance Rate:
56%

Total Applicants:
11,305

Total Acceptances:
6,370

Freshman Enrollment:
1,550

Yield (percentage of admitted students who actually enroll):
24%

Early Decision Available?
Yes

Early Action Available?
No

Total Early Decision Applicants:
309

Total Early Decision Acceptances:
154

Early Decision Deadline:
November 1

Early Decision Notification:
December 15

Regular Decision Deadline:
March 1

Regular Decision Notification:
April 15

Must Reply-By Date:
May 1

Common Application Accepted?
Yes

Supplemental Forms?
Yes

Admissions Phone:
(800) 429-4274

Admissions E-mail:
admission@ithaca.edu

Admissions Website:
http://www.ithaca.edu/admission

SAT I or ACT Required?
Either

First-Year Students Submitting SAT Scores:
98%

SAT I Range (25th – 75th Percentile):
1090-1270

SAT I Verbal Range (25th – 75th Percentile):
540-630

SAT I Math Range (25th – 75th Percentile):
550-640

Retention Rate:
87.5%

Top 10% of High School Class:
36%

Application Fee:
$55

Financial Information

Tuition:
$22,264

Room and Board:
$9,466

Books and Supplies:
$906

Average Need-Based Financial Aid Package (including loans, work-study, grants, and other sources):
$19,627 per year

Students Who Applied For Financial Aid:
77%

Students Who Applied For Financial Aid and Received It:
90%

Early Decision Deadlines

Complete CSS Profile Application:
November 1

File FAFSA form with Dept. of Education:
February 1

Enrollment Advance Deposit:
February 1

File Express TAP (NY Residents) with HESC:
May 1

Submit Stafford Loan Request Form (LRF):
June 1

Regular Decision Deadlines

File FAFSA form with Dept. of Education:
February 1

File express TAP (NY Residents) with HESC:
May 1

Enrollment Advance Deposit:
May 1

Stafford Load Request Form (LRF):
June 1

Financial Aid Phone:
(607) 274-3131

Financial Aid E-mail:
finaid@ithaca.edu

Financial Aid Website:
http://www.ithaca.edu/finaid

Academics

The Lowdown On...
Academics

Degrees Awarded:
Bachelor's

Master's

Most Popular Areas of Study:
Television-Radio

Music

Business Administration and Management

Physical Therapy/Therapist

Sociology

Undergraduate Schools:
Roy H. Park School of Communications

School of Business

School of Health Sciences and Human Performance

School of Humanities and Sciences

School of Music

Fulltime Faculty:
440

Faculty with Terminal Degree:
89%

Student-to-Faculty Ratio:
12:1

Average Course Load:
Five

Special Degree Options:
Planned Studies Program

Pre-law Advisory

Pre-medical Sciences Advisory

Health Sciences Pre-professional

Gerontology Institute

Cross-registration with Cornell University and Wells College

3-2 engineering programs with Cornel

Accelerated programs with Pennsylvania College of Optometry and State University of New York College of Optometry

Special Degree Options
(*Cont'd*)...
One year M.B.A. program

New York State teacher certification programs in art education

Health

Physical education

English

French

German

Spanish

Mathematics

Social studies

Teaching students with speech and language disabilities

Music

Biology

Chemistry

Physics

Sample Academic Clubs:
Public Relations Student Society of America

Students in Free Enterprise

International Business Association

Art History Club

Best Places to Study

The Pub, which is located in the Campus Center, the top floor of the library, and when the weather is nice, outside on the Quad.

Did You Know?
• Ithaca College was recently ranked **seventh** among regional colleges and universities in the north.

• In a study called "Project Connect," consisting of nearly 4,000 college-bound high school students from across the United States, students rated Ithaca as **the "best" in the northern region** of the United States.

• Ithaca was founded in 1892 as the **Ithaca Conservatory of Music** and located in downtown Ithaca until the 1960s.

• Ninety-eight percent of Ithaca graduates are employed and/ or attending graduate school **within a year of graduation.**

Students Speak Out On...
Academics

> "I love my classes, especially those in my major—Organizational Communication, Learning, and Design. The professors are great, they lead interesting classes, and are really friendly and accessible."

Q "**Most all of my classes are interesting**; the professors are very helpful and always willing to spend extra time with you."

Q "Most of the professors I've had are extremely nice and easy to talk to. For the most part I've personally only taken classes I was interested in, so I found them enjoyable. Of course, there are exceptions to both of these rules, but **overall the professors and classes are great."**

Q "The professors really vary. **I've had some great ones, and some that aren't so great.** Overall, though, the professors I've had really seem to love what they do, which is a definite plus. For the most part my classes are interesting, and although I've had the occasional boring one, I'm usually entertained enough to go every class."

Q "Most of the professors I've had are caring, active in the community, spunky, knowledgeable, and politically liberal. Classes? **A good mixture between interesting and challenging."**

Q "**Ninety percent of the classes I can say I learned something from,** which is the true measure of success for me. Most of my history and journalism professors I know outside of the classroom."

Q **"Some professors treat their classes like high school,** but for the most part the professors are interested in relaying the information. It's up to the student to not let apathy from other students interfere with the classroom atmosphere."

Q "After four years at IC and taking classes in each school except for the business school, I've found that the professors range from excellent to mediocre. **I've found all of my classes interesting** because learning new things, in and of itself, is interesting and most of my professors keep the material from being dry if it shows potential."

Q "I am a television-radio major, so I find that most of my professors are pretty amazing. Most of the teachers that I've had don't harp on perfection at all. They really care that we learn the material and give hands-on training with the equipment right away, which is what makes this school so great. When I took a tour of this school, the fact that they offered hands-on experience your first semester here really made Ithaca stand out in my mind. In addition, **you could work on ICTV shows that are totally student run and broadcasted to the county on Time Warner Cable.** However, there are a few professors (all colleges have this) that seem very unapproachable and a bit intimidating at times."

Q "Some of the professors that I've had are really good, while others are boring or hard graders. Some post notes and other helpful things online, but they are not substitutes for going to class! Most classes are interesting, but **I recommend going to your professor's office hours no matter how you're doing in the class**, because it can never hurt you or your grade to know the professor on a first hand basis."

Q "It depends on the courses you're taking. Most classes are interesting, but **the professors can sometimes be a bit unnerving**, especially in courses that deal with politics and history."

Q "Professors and classes are really hit and miss. I have had some professors who are absolutely amazing, and made class so much fun while simultaneously teaching me more than I thought I could learn. On the other hand, I have had awful professors and teachers. **My advice: avoid tenured professors!"**

Q "Professors are cordial, and **Ithaca College's size allows for close personal interaction** and contact whenever necessary."

Q "I have not come across one professor that I haven't liked. Professors at Ithaca look for methods of teaching that make classes fun and interesting. They go far beyond what is required of them and what a textbook would teach. I look forward to every class for one reason or another. One word that stands out when it comes to professors and courses at Ithaca College is 'creative.' **Each class is distinctly its own.** Most of the courses that I have taken here focus on group projects, presentations, and writing, which are the key skills that most of us will need in our future careers."

Q "**I find my professors to be very accommodating.** If they don't have office hours that I am able to attend, I usually find that they are more than willing to meet outside of the posted hours."

Q "Many of the classes are interesting, but as I am sure is the case everywhere, **the quality of professor varies from one to another."**

Q "Although I am only a freshman, throughout the semester and a half I have attended classes I have gotten to know a few of my professors quite well. One professor, in fact, after one brief conversation, asked me to write a research paper to be **submitted to a national conference in New Mexico."**

The College Prowler Take On...
Academics

The music, communications, and physical therapy programs at IC have great reputations. With the exploratory major, students who have yet to decide on a major can take a variety of classes to try to gauge their interests. For those who want to design a major, Ithaca offers a planned studies option where the student works with an adviser to design his or her program of choice. IC also has numerous study abroad programs and centers in London, Los Angeles, and Washington, D.C. Students find their classes taught by professors who have practiced in their field. Most faculty members either have worked in their teaching field or have done extensive research or written books in their field of expertise. All professors have office hours, and many students utilize these times to ask questions and get feedback on their work.

With the atmosphere of a small liberal arts college, Ithaca offers a world of possibilities. First-year seminar classes help turn high school seniors into college freshmen, and internships help students get experience in the working world. Through it all, the faculty and staff at IC is ready to assist their students. It is possible to become friends with professors while attending IC, and most students know as least one professor personally by the time that they graduate. Once you're a student, the best thing to do is to have an upperclassman advise you on the classes to take. It's a good chance that they have either taken the professor for class, or know someone that has.

The College Prowler™ Grade on
Academics: B

A high Academics grade generally indicates that professors are knowledgeable, accessible, and genuinely interested in their students' welfare. Other determining factors include class size, how well professors communicate, and whether or not classes are engaging.

Local Atmosphere

The Lowdown On...
Local Atmosphere

Region:
Northeast

City, State:
Ithaca, New York

Setting:
Medium-Sized Town

Distance from New York City:
4 hours

Distance from Syracuse:
1 hour

Points of Interest:
Lake Cayuga
Hangar Theatre
Sagan Planet Walk
Ithaca Art Trail
Ringwood Raceway
Kitchen Theatre
Ithaca Farmers Market
Cayuga Wine Trail
Buttermilk Falls State Park
Finger Lakes Wine Trail
Taughannock Falls.

➡

Closest Shopping Malls or Plazas:

Pyramid Mall
DeWitt Mall
Cayuga Mall
Triphammer Mall

Closest Movie Theatres:

331 Cinemapolis
171 East State St.
The Commons Center, Ithaca
Phone: (607) 277-6115

Cornell Cinema
Willard Straight Hall
Cornell University, Ithaca
Phone: (607) 255-3522

Fall Creek Pictures
1201 N. Tioga St., Ithaca
(607) 272-1256

Regal Entertainment Group
Pyramid Mall, Ithaca
(607) 257-2700

Major Sports Teams:

Football:
Buffalo Bills
New York Giants
New York Jets
Buffalo Destroyers (AFL)
New York Dragons (AFL)

Hockey:
Buffalo Sabres
New York Islanders
New York Rangers
Baseball:
New York Mets
New York Yankees

Basketball:
New York Knicks
New York Liberty (WNBA)

Soccer:
Metrostars

City Websites

http://www.visitithaca.com
http://www.theithacajournal.com
http://www.ci.ithaca.ny.us
http://www.ithaca.edu/ithacaguide
http://www.ithacaevents.com
http://www.ithacanet.org
http://www.14850.com

Did You Know?

5 Fun Facts about Ithaca

- Outside Magazine named Ithaca the 14th "Best College Town in the Country."
- Bike Magazine calls Ithaca one of "America's Five Best Mountain Biking Towns."

• From 1910-1920, Wharton Studios made movies in a studio at Stewart Park, in Ithaca.

• Ithaca was named due to its location in the town of Ulysses. The ancient Greek Ulysses lived in the town of Ithaki.

• Ithaca has its own currency, called Ithaca HOURs, which is intended to keep and stimulate business downtown.

Famous People from Ithaca:

Many people who have either lived in Ithaca or attended IC or Cornell have made significant impacts on the local area, as well as the world. Some of these individuals include:

- **Ruth Bader Ginsburg**, U.S. Supreme Court Justice, Cornell class of '54
- **Alex Haley**, author of "Roots"
- **Robert Trent Jones**, designed more than 400 of the world's golf courses, attended Cornell
- **Bill Nye**, science media host and other, Cornell class of '77
- **Roy H. Park**, namesake of IC Communications school, media giant, launched Duncan Hines
- **Christopher Reeve**, actor, activist for medical research, Cornell class of '74
- **Janet Reno**, former U.S. attorney general, Cornell class of '60
- **Carl Sagan**, famous astronomer, Cornell professor
- **Rod Serling**, creator of "The Twilight Zone," taught at IC
- **E.B. White**, author, Cornell class of '21
- **Paul Wolfowitz**, Deputy Secretary of Defense, Cornell class of '65

Local Slang

Collegetown: Area near Cornell University. The streets are lined with shops, restaurants, and bars.

The Commons: A pedestrian marketplace which is the home to many boutiques and restaurants.

Cornellian: A person who attends Cornell.

East Hill: The hill on which Cornell is located.

Ithaca is Gorges: Referring to Ithaca's many natural gorges, this phrase is most commonly seen on clothing and bumper stickers.

Ithacan: An IC student, also the name of the college newspaper.

South Hill: The hill on which IC is located.

Ten Square Miles Surrounded By Reality: Another common bumper sticker, referring to Ithaca's unique atmosphere. People will also call Ithaca "the bubble," referring to the idea that Ithaca is in its own world.

"It is nice to have Cornell nearby because you can easily visit the other campus if you want to. Ithaca is very much a college town, so you can always find students downtown hanging out in the Commons."

Q "Ithaca is very friendly. I was pleasantly surprised after coming here from a big city. There isn't really one dominant type of person or clique, which is very nice and refreshing. **I have yet to encounter someone from Cornell,** but it's pretty to visit and nice to know it's so close. Definitely hike around at least one gorge and get friendly with the 24-hour Wegmans."

Q "The atmosphere is alright. Cornell is a great resource to have nearby. **It is a great place if you enjoy nature."**

Q "The atmosphere is cool. Most of the people are chill and fun to get to know. **Having Cornell nearby just means there's more stuff to do in town.** Otherwise, it doesn't really affect us. Definitely visit all the waterfalls. They are absolutely beautiful, even when they're frozen in the winter."

Q "Take advantage of hiking before it gets really cold. If you like movies, **there are great theatres in town,** like Fall Creek Pictures, Cinemapolis, and Cornell Cinema. The downtown Commons is really cool too, if you like that kind of thing."

Q "**Ithaca is a medium-sized town with highly liberal leanings.** During the beginning of the War on Iraq in March 2003, parking garages were spray-painted with 'Bush is a Nazi,' and anti-war demonstrations were held weekly from September through March. Aside from the political leanings, however, Ithaca is a great small-town, with tons of shops and restaurants, and plenty of unique places to spend an afternoon or evening."

Q **"The atmosphere is very laid-back and laissez-faire**. It's great to have a huge university on the other hill because it provides many more opportunities for cultural learning, socializing, and intense academic study. Definitely visit the gorges, Buttermilk Falls, Treman Park, and the Commons."

Q "Cornell is a great resource for classes and for research. Being in a two-college town, most things in Ithaca are geared toward students, which creates a great atmosphere. **There are beautiful waterfalls, parks, and great hiking."**

Q "The atmosphere is great. It's the main reason I chose Ithaca over any other college. There are always things to do, aside from partying, like visiting parks in the fall or going sledding in the winter. **The Commons is a great place where you can find many different types of food.** Having Cornell nearby definitely enhances the community with the amount of students it brings to the area, increasing business and available choices for shopping, eating, and extracurricular activities."

Q "You definitely have to visit the Farmers Market and Taughannock Falls. The college is also set on a hill with a beautiful view overlooking Cayuga Lake. **Every time I look at it I get a sense of pride and pleasure** to be gaining a degree in such a fantastic location."

Q "One of Ithaca's downfalls is the fact that it's a very isolated campus. It's built on a hill, which means that we receive more wind than Cornell does. **It's almost like being in two different places.** I don't really go to Cornell much, but I think that a major draw of having Cornell around for IC students is the Greek life that Ithaca doesn't have. A majority of students enjoy partying at Cornell on the weekends. One nice thing is that IC students can take classes at Cornell."

Q "Ithaca College is pretty removed from Ithaca proper, especially in the winter. **Campus politics are very liberal,** but thankfully, many people are too concerned with their daily lives and activities to care whether or not you're a Republican, Democrat, or of any political affiliation, for that matter. Cornell parties are great, but you grow out of them after awhile."

Q "It's Hippy USA, but a really great place to go to school. If you are from a small, conservative, rural town like me, Ithaca is a complete 180, but it makes for a great school environment. **Stay away from the Triphammer Mall!** Stay away from the Dewitt Mall for that matter, too, unless you want to go to Moosewood. Go to the parks, Treman, Buttermilk, etc. They are gorges!"

Q " Having Cornell nearby is probably beneficial in ways that I don't even realize. It provides twice as many opportunities for people. Now, as far as things that you should see: **even if you aren't a nature person, the scenery is amazing.** A lot of it you don't even have to hike to, if that's not your thing. For instance, Ithaca Falls, a waterfall that compares and surpasses many falls I have seen in places like Hawaii, is on my way to the mall. Other places, like Truman Park, everyone should see. Of course, those aren't things that you are going to see everyday, but the town is pretty fun in itself. I am not much of a partier, but the people are so cool and interesting. Hanging out in the Commons on a nice day is really great."

Q "The atmosphere at Ithaca is comfortable and friendly. **People are free to dress, act, speak, and be exactly who they are**, and the many diverse clubs that we have on campus demonstrate this. Each year new clubs and activities are created to appeal to all of the different hobbies and interests of the students. The faculty and staff of Ithaca College is incredibly friendly. An example is the dining halls—not only do I love the food, but the chefs are always smiling and doing their best to make you feel at home. Little things like conversations with Horace, one of the omelet chefs, can really make my day."

Q "Cornell is a wonderful resource for both academics and social life. Cornell is very open to Ithaca students, whether they want to find out more about a program or department, or if they would like to join forces for an event or cause. One of the greatest things about this town is that **there's so much going on.** I have been able to explore many different activities going on in Ithaca, and have learned so much about different people, their ways of life and what they do for fun. Depending on where you look, you can find both a small town atmosphere that is intimate and tightly knit, as well as a typical college town with all amenities necessary including bars, shopping centers and restaurants."

Q **"Ithaca leans toward the liberal side, hence plenty of homosexuals and "hippies."** Cornell can be good because you can party there or go see the good bands that come to perform, like Counting Crows last year. However, they tend to be kind of snotty and I have to say, not too good looking either. The downtown Commons is pretty nice, cute, quaint, etc. There are lots of cool little shops. Definitely go to the Applefest in the autumn in the Commons. The gorges are also pretty cool, but you have to make sure you go there early in the year, because as soon as it gets cold you won't be able to go. There are a few within walking distance of campus and people often go cliff-jumping and swimming in them, or just hike to them for their simple beauty."

Q "The Cornell rivalry is fun; **Collegetown is a nice break from the Commons and vice versa**. The different environments, so close to one another, provide variety and changes of pace if you so desire."

Q "I love having Cornell nearby, because you get the small college perks (smaller classes, more one-on-one interaction with professors, getting to know more people, tighter knit community) while still getting the larger, college town atmosphere, because at all the clubs, restaurants, and off-campus activities there are Cornellians as well as Ithacans, and **it's really nice to continue to get to know lots of** people and not feel restricted by the small number at IC."

Q "Overall, it has been difficult for me to find people that are hard to be around. Most everyone makes you feel comfortable being around them. I think the atmosphere at the college is conducive to that—not too small, not too big. **Cornell is a great resource to have.** For many people, it is an outlet on the weekends for partying purposes, but for other reasons, such as athletic events, academic resources, and concerts, Cornell is a great neighbor to have."

The College Prowler Take On...
Local Atmosphere

Ithaca, with a population of 29,000, is the home to both IC and Cornell University. With quaint little coffee houses, excellent theaters, large used bookstores, happening bars and dance clubs, boutiques and shops selling everything from the hottest fashions to the perfect bumper sticker, there's always something to do or see in Ithaca. In the midst of it all is the Commons, a marketplace with restaurants, outside entertainment, and specialty stores. Collegetown, located next to the Cornell campus, also has a variety of different places to eat and shop. Around Lake Cayuga, tourists and wine enthusiasts follow the Finger Lakes Wine Trail, a series of local wineries that offer samples of their specialties. It's hard to walk around campus or go downtown and not see someone with an "Ithaca is Gorges" shirt. No, Ithacans can spell, it's just that Ithaca really is "gorges." Ithaca and the surrounding areas' numerous streams have cut deep ravines and gorges into the hillsides, all of which lead to the lake. One of the most spectacular sights is Taughannock Falls, which boasts the highest free-falling waterfalls in the eastern United States, even higher than Niagara Falls. Countless other waterfalls and ravines dot the surrounding areas, and on a warm day, students can be found enjoying picnics, swimming, and hiking on picturesque trails.

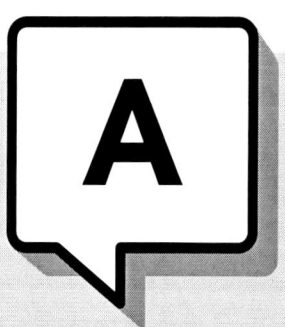

The College Prowler™ Grade on

Local Atmosphere: A

A high Local Atmosphere grade indicates that the area surrounding campus is safe and scenic. Other factors include nearby attractions, proximity to other schools, and the town's attitude toward students

Safety & Security

The Lowdown On...
Safety & Security

Number of IC Police:
18

Phone:
911 (emergencies)
(607) 274-3333 (non-emergencies)

Safety Services:
24-Hour foot and vehicle patrols
Late night transport and escort service
24-Hour emergency telephones
Lighted pathways and sidewalks
Student patrols
Controlled dormitory access (key security card, etc)
Motorist assistance program

Health Center Office Hours:
Monday-Friday, 8 a.m- 4.p.m., and emergency care is available 24 hours a day

Health Services

Hammond Health Center offers primary and emergency care, overnight care, sports medicine, specialist referrals, prescription refills, allergy shots, gynecology and women's care, birth control, and HIV testing

Did You Know?

There are seventy-six **blue light phones** on the campus and an emergency phone is located at each of the three college directional maps. All seventy-six phones are tested weekly.

• The sworn officers at IC are **certified by New York,** and the officers' training is the same as any municipal police officer or county sheriff deputy.

Students Speak Out On...
Safety & Security

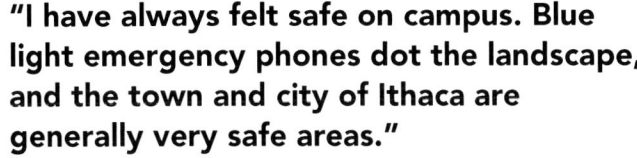

"I have always felt safe on campus. Blue light emergency phones dot the landscape, and the town and city of Ithaca are generally very safe areas."

Q "I have never felt unsafe; everything is well-lit and very comfortable."

Q "There are blue lights in lots of places, but I don't see too many police around."

Q "I haven't really had to use any of their services, but they seem pretty good. I'm not sure, but when my car battery needed a jump once, the campus police were very helpful."

Q "It's excellent. Student officers walk through all the residence halls at night and Public Safety is usually very quick to respond to emergencies."

Q "Campus Safety is always around. I have seen them driving around on campus at all hours of the day and night. If you ever need help, the officers are really nice. I have never felt unsafe on campus, even when walking home from the newspaper at 3 a.m."

Q "Security is great. I've never had any problems when I've needed assistance on campus, and parking services, i.e. those who write parking tickets, are so quick, I've never missed earning a ticket when I've deserved one."

Q "Public Safety is always around. **There are blue lights everywhere that you could use if you needed them**, but I feel safe enough on the campus to walk around at night, even if I'm by myself."

Q **"Ithaca College is by far one of the safest places I've ever been in my life."**

Q "OK, it could be better lit, but **it is a safe campus, except when your cars get egged."**

Q **"Everywhere you look there is a blue light**. I don't know; I have never felt like I couldn't walk around by myself even after dark."

Q "Campus Safety is a professional, friendly group of officers that patrol and take things seriously. **Everyone feels safe**, and there is an abundance of safety phones in case of emergency."

Q "Ithaca College takes safety on campus very seriously. I have always felt secure. When I walk back from the library or another dorm late at night, blue emergency lights are always visible in every direction that I look. **I also see police cars driving around at all hours of the night to assure everyone's safety.** When a crime is committed, action is taken immediately and the proper precautions are taken so that it does not happen again."

Q "For the most part, I feel really safe on campus. I have never worried about walking back to my room even at 3 a.m., though **I do keep my eyes open on the weekends when the drunks are out."**

Q "**I feel safe on campus all the time**. I frequently find myself walking alone on campus because of various meetings and such, but never feel threatened and uncomfortable when I do so."

The College Prowler Take On...
Safety & Security

When looking out over the campus landscape at night, you will find blue emergency phones scattered all around the campus, and most students say they have never felt unsafe at IC. While the Ithaca area is a relatively safe place to be, the eighteen public safety officers work hard to keep the campus secure. To keep everyone informed of the incidents that required public safety involvement, the college newspaper, The Ithacan, runs a weekly public safety log which includes what officers responded to in the last week. If someone doesn't feel comfortable walking around campus at night, the colleges Student Auxiliary Safety Patrol assists students in getting where they need to be, and dorms are locked after 9 p.m. and can only be entered by a resident with his or her key.

IC has a very low crime rate, and the public safety staff takes every precaution to keep it that way. Once a student calls with a problem, the officers are very responsive, and they don't take any issue lightly. The only real problems the campus community has seen in the past year were incidents of car vandalism. This is a case where students need to use common sense. Valuables such as money, jewelry, or laptops should always be safeguarded. Some students have the opinion that public safety officers are just trying to ruin weekend fun, but the officers' goal is to protect the campus community. The dedicated staff tries to protect students from being victims or taking part in reckless behavior. All in all, most students think that that there are few places that exist where people can feel safer.

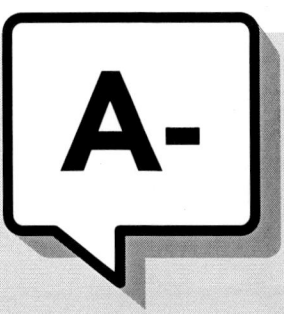

The College Prowler™ Grade on

Safety & Security: A-

A high grade in Safety & Security means that students generally feel safe, campus police are visible, blue-light phones and escort services are readily available, and safety precautions are not overly necessary.

Computers

The Lowdown On...
Computers

High-Speed Network?
Yes

Numbers of Computers:
624

Wireless Network?
No

Operating Systems:
PC
MAC

Number of Labs:
30

24-Hour Labs:
Friends 110
West Tower

Free Software

Adobe Acrobat Reader, Aladdin Expander, WS_FTP, Fetch, JInitiator, Macintosh Runtime for Java, McAfee VirusScan and VirusScan Definition Update (Windows), Virex and Virex Definition Update (Macintosh), CorporateTime, Advance 6.1

Discounted Software

The main software applications used on campus include the Microsoft Office suite (for both Windows and Macintosh), Microsoft Internet Explorer, and Netscape Communicator. Software can be purchased at educational prices from the bookstore or from many retailers and mail order companies. All you need to do is identify yourself as a college student or employee to receive special academic pricing.

Charge to Print?

Dot matrix printing is provided at no charge. Laser printing is available to students for a $10 per semester fee. Stop by the bookstore to fill out a laser printing request form.

Did You Know?

The Computer Science club has a **website!** Unfortunately, it hasn't been updated since November of 2001. Irony at its finest.

Students Speak Out On...
Computers

"Bring a computer. There are labs, but they are a pain and hold weird hours. ResNet (the campus-wide network) could be better, but when it works it's pretty fast."

Q "**The labs are usually crowded,** but I've never been unable to find a computer. I recommend having your own computer so you can do work in the privacy of your own room. Also, one of the staples of college life is AOL Instant Messenger, and you'd need your own computer for that. Plus, it's just cool to have your own computer so you can play games or whatnot."

Q "The computer network is awful. They claim to be trying to fix it, and that downloading is the problem, but that's a lie. It's better than it was before, though. I don't really use the computer labs. Students should bring their own computers. The library is good about printing and having programs on their computers and stuff, **but it's hard to find a free computer in there.** You can survive without a computer of your own, but you might not be happy that you did."

Q "The computer network connection on campus is terrible. The Ethernet connection drops on a fairly regular basis. Students don't absolutely need a computer, but **lab space is tough to get during finals week."**

Q "The network has sucked lately. **Some professors have set up course software that students can access through any computer on campus.** Bring your own computer, but print at the labs."

Q "The few times I have tried to use the labs, they have been consistently crowded. I would recommend students bring their own computers, because so much stuff relating to this college and classwork is found online, such as the online student directory for people's phone numbers, registration for classes, and some class syllabi. It also helps because **only one lab on campus is open 24 hours, but the printer in that lab stops at 11 p.m.**, which is not very convenient if you are finishing your term paper at 2 a.m. As far as the network is concerned, the college has been trying to improve it constantly. Between computer viruses that make a mess of e-mails to music file-sharing programs, the network can get slow at times. It's faster than the dial-up I have at home, though."

Q "**The computer labs and library are crowded during certain key hours**. Find out when those hours are, steer clear during those hours, and you're set for four years."

Q "It's always helpful for students to bring their own computer. During the final weeks the labs are always overcrowded. Besides that, just the convenience factor is enough. **The weather deters students from doing a lot of things,** and walking to the computer lab maybe one of them. ResNet, our internet connection, isn't too great. Partly I feel that it's because students are file sharing, so it slows our connection speed down and spreads a lot of viruses."

Q "Computers are new and up-to-date. **It's hard to get a computer in the lab or in the library during certain hours of the day** though, because of the convenience of using them in between classes."

Q "Although computer labs usually don't exceed capacity, **a personal computer is strongly recommended**. We have a 24-hour computer lab, but you are only able to print until 11 p.m., and being able to work in the peace and quiet of your own room is a plus."

Q "I guess I would say that having my own computer is a great thing, but it's not necessary. **A lot of my projects for classes have to be done on a Mac**, so I use labs, and I don't mind it at all. Nothing is too far away, and there are a lot of places you can go."

Q "The computer network, despite recent problems, is fast and convenient. Computer labs are usually open and not crowded, except around finals and registration time. **Students should bring their own computer if able."**

Q "The computer network has its problems, but that is normal in any environment these days. Recently, I have been in the computer labs three times a day, and I can always find a seat. **The computer services department is very helpful,** and they keep the technology updated. I suggest that students do bring their own computers just because of the nature of the college world. We live in a world where information is updated every second, and to be the best student, you would want to have that information available to you at any time."

Q "I would recommend that students bring their own computer. I find it very convenient to have both a laptop and a printer in my dorm room. I don't have to worry about getting to the computer lab to print out papers, and **I can bring my laptop to class or the library when I need it."**

Q "**ResNet works most of the time,** but it's a source of great frustration for many students, and they're hoping to make it better. Although the computer labs are nice and there are plenty of them, it's much more convenient to have your own computer in your room."

Q "Students should bring their own computers. The labs usually are crowded and **the network is often excruciatingly slow."**

Q "I don't use the computer labs. **I own my own laptop, and I would highly recommend doing the same**. I take my laptop with me to the library, or to meetings to type up notes or papers. It's really handy to have something that's portable."

Q "My experience with the network, ResNet, has been poor and most students would agree with me about this. The moment I stepped on campus in August, we were informed that the network was down due to a virus, and all computers had to be disinfected before the network was turned back on. Throughout the following months **the network was constantly faced with problems,** which caused headaches to many people."

Q "Whenever I go to the computer lab **there's usually at least one computer open.** However, that computer may be a PC and supposedly you have to pay $10 in order to print from a PC in the computer labs, so therefore I recommend Macs in the labs. I think students should bring their own computer. I would be lost without mine because I do all of my homework on it, check my e-mail on an obsessive basis, and also stay connected with people."

The College Prowler Take On...
Computers

It's extremely frustrating to need research for a paper that's due the next day only to find out that ResNet, the campus network, is down. ResNet usually goes down weekly, and in an age where students use AOL Instant Messenger to make plans for dinner instead of walking down the hall to their friend's rooms, the absence of the Internet can almost be debilitating. In the classroom, many professors utilize the technology available to them, and some post homework assignments on a course website called Blackboard, which is an interactive program accessible from any computer with the Internet. Every student receives an e-mail account, and it's usually necessary to check it a few times each day. While most students bring their own computer with them to IC, it's not necessary to have one because of the many computers on campus.

The Office of Information Technology Services tells students they will find a solution to the network problem quickly, and when it does work, it usually works well. IC is also starting to make plans for a campus-wide wireless network that prospective students may have a chance of utilizing in the near future. For $10 a semester, you can buy laser printing privileges at the labs, so if you worry about the high cost of printer ink cartridges, just go to a lab when you need to print something. A couple labs are open around the clock, which is very convenient for procrastinators.

The College Prowler™ Grade on

Computers: C+

A high grade in Computers designates that computer labs are available, the computer network is easily accessible, and the campus' computing technology is up-to-date.

Facilities

The Lowdown On...
Facilities

Student Center:
Movie Theatre on Campus?
No, but films are shown almost
every weekend in Textor Hall.

Bowling on Campus?
No

Bar on Campus?
No

**Coffeehouse on
Campus?**
Yes, La Vincita, in the "alcohol-
free" Pub in the Campus
Center.

Student Center:
The Campus Center

Athletic Center:
The Fitness Center

Libraries:
1

Popular Places to Chill:
The Pub

What Is There to Do?

From grabbing some coffee, watching a film on the weekend, listening to a speaker or attending an IC AfterDark Event, most students can find something to do on campus. IC doesn't have the many amenities that larger schools offer, but with the surrounding city, no student ever has the excuse that he or she can't find something to do.

Favorite Things to Do

Many students enjoy going to concerts at the music school or plays done by the theater department. The college brings in many speakers and performers which also bode well with students. The campus group IC AfterDark sponsors themed-nights on the weekends as an alternative to alcohol, which are always well attended by students.

Students Speak Out On...
Facilities

{ **"The gym is probably the gem of campus facilities, but everything is well-maintained and convenient. The library is especially useful for studying and reflection."**

Q "I think the facilities are exactly what is needed for a college of this size. Athletics are good. There is an awesome fitness center, and computer labs are alright, although I would like to see newer computers in all the labs. **The campus center is great for our size campus."**

Q "The student center could use more places to 'hang out,' but there are conference rooms and TV rooms which help. Also, the activity center is a nice idea and can be fun to play pool and ping pong, but **it should be bigger.** The gym is pretty good; they have a nice selection of things to do with relatively ample locker rooms."

Q "The Fitness Center is nice. It's huge and has a lot of good equipment. The computers in Park (those are the only public ones I really use) are really nice. The ones in the library are OK; they serve their purpose, but are sometimes slow. **The student center is OK**. The game room's not too bad. It would be nice to have a more private place to hang out on campus that aren't loud like the Pub. Overall, for a college this size, the campus center's not too bad."

Q "The gym is great—better than my gym at home in Pittsburgh. There are plenty of elliptical machines, treadmills, and bicycles, as well as weight machines and a large free weight area. **The non-alcoholic Pub is one of the best student-gathering places on campus**. Students often meet there for coffee, sandwiches, or breakfast, and it is also a popular place for groups to meet to complete group projects."

Q "The Fitness Center is great, and the computer labs have the newest computers, but **the Campus Center is a little older and the facilities aren't wonderful**. It's a warm place to meet and hang out with friends."

Q "The common facilities are pretty nice. **The Fitness Center is about five years old**, and the computers are cycled out every three years in most buildings."

Q "The Fitness Center is state of the art: all new cardio-machines, weight machines are always kept in good working order, classes are offered in yoga, tai-chi, pilates, and cardio-kickboxing. If the fitness center does not offer something and you want it, you can request it. Chances are, your request will be granted within a year if interest is fairly high. **There are also several intramural sports and club sports offered to any student who is interested.** You could play intramural floor hockey, outdoor soccer, badminton, basketball, or club tap dancing, ice hockey, or ultimate frisbee!"

Q "I don't like our student center at all. It's too small, and the space is very limited. The interior design of the building isn't visually appealing. The brown is very faded and not pleasant to look at. Our actual student center is very tiny and sometimes I feel it may limit the students and their capabilities. The coffee Pub is a good place to lounge out, relax, or study. **I think one of the best facilities we have on campus is the gym.**"

Q "The Fitness Center is very nice. It is very modern because it was recently completed. However, there are certain times of the day when it is very crowded and you have to wait for machines. The student center is also pretty nice. **Many students like to meet up in the Pub to eat and do work together."**

Q "Ithaca College has top of the line facilities. Our computer labs have recently been upgraded to brand new computers, our gym is full of exercise machines, and our student center, well, it has a big screen TV. **What more could you ask for?"**

Q "At a first glance, the architecture of this campus is rather dull and outdated. However, **when you enter the buildings and classrooms, they're comfortable and technologically advanced.** To me, it's not what's on the outside that counts. The facilities are always clean. The gym is absolutely beautiful, and there is enough equipment and space for basketball, dancing, yoga, etc., for everyone to enjoy a good workout. The facilities available to students are adequate for any event, and with the right décor they are perfect for whatever the occasion may be."

The College Prowler Take On...
Facilities

At first glance, many of the buildings on campus seem like a flashback to the disco era. Most buildings on campus were built in the 1960s and 1970s, and some of their styles show their age. The Quads are the ugliest buildings on campus. Their cement and faded mint-green color combination is very unappealing to the eye. One campus bright spot is outside of Dillingham, the theater building, where beautiful fountains spray high into the air, but they are only on during the summer up until fall break. IC doesn't have the prestigious, historical looking buildings that other universities have because of the overall newness of the campus, but most of the classrooms are state-of-the-art. The Center for Natural Sciences has extensive laboratories, and the Center for Health Sciences has a speech and hearing clinic, physical and occupational therapy clinics, and a wellness center. The Roy H. Park School of Communications has a wealth of resources for media students, including editing labs, studios, and dark rooms. The Writing Center, where students can get assistance in writing and editing papers, is also in Park. Whalen Center for Music has recording facilities and practice rooms, and the college even has an observatory which was the perfect place to go and look at the Mars this past year. Smiddy Hall houses the Center for Trading & Analysis of Financial Instruments, and the lag time between the New York Stock Exchange and IC's trading data is only one-fourth of a second.

The College Prowler™ Grade on

Facilities: B+

A high Facilities grade indicates that the campus is aesthetically pleasing and well-maintained; facilities are state-of-the-art, and libraries are exceptional. Other determining factors include the quality of both athletic and student centers and an abundance of things to do on campus.

Campus Dining

The Lowdown On...
Campus Dining

Freshman Meal Plan Requirement?

Yes

Meal Plan Average Cost:

$4,664

Places to Grab a Bite with Your Meal Plan

Campus Center Dining Hall

Location: Bottom Floor, the Campus Center

Food: Classics, Vegetarian, International, Pizza, Soup and Salad, Grill, Vegan, Sandwiches

Favorite Dish: Soft-Serve Ice Cream, Chicken Nuggets, Special Sauce for Grill Items

Hours: Monday-Thursday 7 a.m.-7:30 p.m., Friday 7 a.m.-6:30 p.m., Saturday 8:30 a.m.-6:30 p.m., Sunday 10:30 a.m.-6:30 p.m.

→

Terrace Dining Hall

Location: Under Terrace 1

Food: Classics, Soup and Salad, Sandwiches, Pizza and Pasta Bar, Vegetarian, Kosher

Favorite Dish: Kosher, Wraps, Italian Bar

Hours: Monday-Thursday 11 a.m.-8 p.m., Friday 11 a.m.-7 p.m., Saturday noon-7 p.m., Sunday noon- 8 p.m.

The Towers

Location: Towers Concourse

Food: Classics, Soup and Salad, Pizza, Grill, Vegetarian, Asian, Dessert Bar

Favorite Dish: Chicken Patty Sandwiches, Macaroni and Cheese

Hours: Monday-Thursday 7 a.m.-7 p.m., 8 p.m.-12 a.m., Friday 7 a.m.-2 p.m.

24-Hour On-Campus Eating?

No

Student Favorites:

The Terraces

La Vincita

Did You Know?

For calorie-counting students and those who don't want to gain the infamous "freshman 15," the **nutrition facts** of all food served in the dining halls are right next to the menu items.

Other Options

You can use your bonus bucks (you get $200 with a fourteen meals per week plan) at BJ's Sub Connection, Campus Center Food Court, La Vincita, Grand Central Café, Tower Club, a full service restaurant on the 14th floor of the East Tower, and at the convenience store, Mac's.

Students Speak Out On...
Campus Dining

"The dining halls have pretty good food considering, but don't go at peak hours or you will get trampled. Hang out in the Pub if you want to pretend to study and look cool."

Q "**Dining halls are OK.** I don't eat in them; I only take my food to go."

Q "Terrace Dining Hall is really good, and there's a large variety of food. Towers is also pretty good. **I personally do not like the Campus Center's food**, but as the name says, it's in the middle of the campus so it's the most convenient. The Pub is also another great place on campus for food, and you can get some work done there too."

Q "The food's actually not that bad, until you start realizing that they serve you the same menus every week. But if you don't mind a lack in variety, the food could definitely be a lot worse. **The food court is expensive,** but the food's usually pretty good. Overall, Terrace Dining Hall is the best. They have the best variety."

Q "The dining halls have gotten steadily worse each year that I've been here. Food is best at the Terrace Dining Hall and worst at Campus Center Dining Hall. **Thankfully, there are plenty of places to order from.**"

Q "Food's not bad. Usually there are plenty of options for vegetarians and vegans. **There are a few staples that are provided every night for dinner** like burgers, pizza, pasta, and sandwiches, and the classic entrees always change. Sometimes those aren't so great, but you get used to it. The quality also depends on which dining hall you eat at. The Terraces generally have better food and a better atmosphere than the Campus Center. We have a good snack bar and a couple of good coffee and smoothie shops on campus where you can use Bonus Bucks. Usually those places offer really yummy options— sushi, Mexican food, hot sandwiches, salads, pastries, snacks, etc."

Q "The food on campus is not bad, compared to other food services. But after two years of eating it, I was ready for a change, and so I moved into an apartment to do my own cooking. **The Terrace Dining Hall has the most selection."**

Q "**The food on campus is great**. You have numerous choices, from vegan to pizza and wings. Milkshakes are served at the Towers Dining Hall. The Campus Center Dining Hall boasts fresh, made-to-order omelets every morning of the week. Lastly, the Terrace Dining Hall always offers sandwich wraps, an Italian bar with sauces, noodles, and garlic bread and ice cream for dessert almost every night."

Q "The food here is OK. It isn't horrible and it isn't great. I just think after eating it for so long I'm very nostalgic towards it. I go to each dining hall for different reasons. **I like eating at the Campus Center for lunch**. Their lunch exhibition cooking is very good. Also I think that they have the best salads on campus. For dinner I like to eat at the West Tower because of their attempt at cooking Chinese food. It makes me feel at home. Terraces, however, has the best variety. They have a pasta bar, Kosher food, exhibition cooking, and sandwich bar."

Q "**Terraces is the best dining hall overall**. Most students like it over the other two, but it also depends on how close you live to it, and what kind of food you're in the mood for."

Q "It varies by dining hall. The Terrace Dining Hall generally serves the best food and has the best atmosphere, but is usually the most crowded. **Campus Center offers a limited selection and seems to cater to vegetarians**, but if you are active on campus, you will probably eat here more than you would like. The Towers Dining Hall is average, but has a great view of Ithaca and Lake Cayuga to look at while you eat."

Q "**Alright, Terraces is the best, but is often crowded**. Campus Center is intolerable for dinner, but they do have soft serve ice cream with toppings, yum!"

Q "I am impressed with the food on campus. Of course they serve a lot of crap that sometimes you need to resist, but they also have options for good food. The best place to eat is supposedly the Terraces, but I find some good stuff in the other places too, and so much variety, which is good for a picky eater like myself. The other option is buying food on campus with bonus bucks, which are a part of your meal plan. My favorite place to go alone or with a friend is the Pub. It's a good atmosphere to talk, do homework in, or play a game of cards. Then you can walk over and get a cup of coffee or whatever you want. **They have the best hot chocolate ever**, by the way!"

Q "**The food on this campus is amazing, period.** I look forward to every meal. In fact, I am going to be a senior next year and I will be staying on campus because I love the food so much! At every meal, there are both old-fashioned American favorites as well as a healthy array of foods. It is always fresh. Plus, the chefs and management do their best to appeal to everyone's tastes. They're always looking for feedback and new ideas to keep the meals different but delicious."

Q **"Both a vegan grill and Kosher dining are available** for students who have certain eating disciplines. The Terrace Dining Hall is known for having the best food and largest selection. The Towers is well known for its Dessert Bar and its Late Night option which runs from 8 p.m. to midnight. I think that the Campus Center is by far the best because the food selection and quality is consistent, and the chefs are the friendliest and treat you like family."

Q "The Terrence Dining Hall is the favorite on campus. It has the most variety. The best advice I received about campus food was that if you eat the same foods all the time then you won't like anything. **Change it up and you won't get sick of it."**

Q "Sorry to say, the food is slowly declining in quality. Campus Center is the most convenient dining hall, but also has the worst food. Terraces has the best food and is kind of neat looking, but if you live further down, then the amount of stairs you have to climb to get to it, especially in winter, sometimes doesn't make it worth the effort. **At least all the dining halls have certain foods you can count on,** like pizza, cereal, sandwiches, and usually good desserts. La Vincita has good stuff, like pizza, hot and cold sandwiches, baked goods, soup, etc."

Q "I think the Terrace Dining Hall is the best college food I've ever had, and I've visited a lot of campuses. I think that between the salad bar, the sandwich bar, the pasta bar, the ice cream bar, the dessert bar and the hot food line, there is a lot of variety. It makes eating in the dining hall a more pleasurable activity than it probably should be at college. Being off campus now, **I really miss those hot, well-balanced meals.** Plus, the food court type atmosphere with the fountain in the Terraces is really nice."

The College Prowler Take On...
Campus Dining

When students find themselves busy studying for tests, sometimes the only social scene the students find is at the dining hall. Ithaca's three dining halls—Campus Center, the Towers, and the Terraces—each provide good atmospheres for conversation and usually a decent meal. The Terrace Dining Hall has by far the best food on campus, but it's the longest walk for most students, and it's usually the busiest as well. The Towers and Campus Center have a grab-and-go lunch option that's great for the students who need to eat a quick lunch or want to take it back to their rooms. The dining halls also have themed meals about once a week, such as Italian or Mexican night. BJ's Convenience Store, located in the Towers Concourse, makes tasty subs and accepts bonus bucks. For the perfect fruit smoothie on one of the warm days in Ithaca, or a cup of coffee when it's terribly cold, stop by the Grand Central Café in the Campus Center.

All in all, campus food is pretty decent. Compared to other schools some students have visited, the food at IC is gourmet. Sometimes what is served in the dining halls seems a bit repetitive, but students find that varying which dining halls they go to or looking at the menus posted online before deciding where they will eat leaves them more satisfied. The dining halls offer everything from steaks and cereal to vegan and Asian. Besides the high price ($4,664 for the 2003-2004 school year), most students are generally pleased with their dining experiences.

B

The College Prowler™ Grade on

Campus Dining: B

Our grade on Campus Dining addresses the quality of both school-owned dining halls and independent on-campus restaurants as well as the price, availability, and variety of food.

Off-Campus Dining

The Lowdown On...
Off-Campus Dining

Restaurant Prowler:
Popular Places to Eat!

ABC Café
Food: Vegetarian
Address: 308 Stewart Ave., Ithaca
Phone: (607) 277-4770
Cool Features: ABC Café is a great place to go for those with special dietary needs. They cater to those with wheat-free and dairy-free preferences.
Price: $7 and under per person
Hours: Monday-Sunday 9:30 a.m.-11 p.m.

Aladdin's Natural Eatery
Food: Greek, Lebanese, Mediterranean
Address: 100 Dryden Road, Ithaca
Phone: (607) 273-5000
Fax: (607) 273-2810
Price: $15 and under per person
Hours: Monday-Thursday 11:30 a.m.-10:30 p.m., Friday 11:30 a.m.-11:30 p.m.

Angelina Centini's
Food: Italian
Address: 124 Coddington Road, Ithaca
Phone: (607) 273-0802
Price: $15 and under per person
Hours: Tuesday-Thursday 5 p.m.-9 p.m., Friday-Saturday 5 p.m.-10 p.m., lunch Tuesday-Friday 11 a.m.-2 p.m.

Antlers
Food: American, seafood
Address: 1159 Dryden Road, Ithaca
Phone: (607) 273-9725
Price: $15 and under per person
Hours: Sunday-Thursday 5 p.m.-9:30 p.m., Friday-Saturday 5 p.m.-10 p.m.

Applebee's
Food: American
Address: 2300 N. Triphammer Rd., Ithaca
Phone: (607) 257-6200
Fax: (607) 257-1905
Price: $15 and under per person
Hours: Sunday-Thursday 11 a.m.-11 p.m., Friday-Saturday 11 a.m.-12 a.m.

Bistro Q
Food: American, barbecue
Address: 708 W. Buffalo St., Ithaca
Phone: (607) 277-3287
Fax: (607) 277-3673
Cool Features: Known for their fantastic barbeque and their big deck which is located on the shore of Lake Cayuga. If you hear a train on the nearby tracks, all drinks are half-off for seventeen minutes.
Price: $15 and under per person
Hours: Tuesday-Thursday 11 a.m.-9 p.m., Friday 11 a.m.-10 p.m., Saturday 10 a.m.-10 p.m., Sunday 10 a.m.-9 p.m.

The Boatyard Grill
Food: American, seafood
Address: 525 Taughannock Blvd., Ithaca
Phone: (607) 256-2628
Price: $20 and under per person
Hours: Monday-Saturday 5 p.m.-10 p.m., Sunday 11 a.m.-10 p.m.

Chili's
Food: Mexican
Address: 608 S. Meadow St., Ithaca
Phone: (607) 272-5004
Fax: (607) 272-6606
Price: $15 and under per person

Chili's (*Continued...*)
Hours: Sunday-Thursday 11 a.m.-11 p.m., Friday-Saturday 11 a.m.-12 a.m.

Collegetown Bagels
Food: Bagels, deli, bakery, coffee, appetizers
Address 1: East Hill Plaza, Ithaca
Phone 1: (607) 273-1036
Hours 1: Monday-Saturday 6 a.m.-7 p.m., Sunday 6:30 a.m.-4 p.m.

Address 2: 203 N. Aurora St., Ithaca
Phone 2: (607) 273-2848
Hours 2: Monday-Saturday 6:30 a.m.-6 p.m., Sunday 6:30 a.m.-5:30 p.m.

Address 3: 415 College Ave., Ithaca
Phone 3: (607) 273-0982
Hours 3: Monday-Sunday 6:30 a.m.-2 a.m.

Address 4: Triphammer Mall, Ithaca
Phone 4: (607) 257-2255
Hours 4: Monday-Saturday 7 a.m.-7:30 p.m., Sunday 7 a.m.-5 p.m.
Price: $5 and under per person

D.P. Dough
Food: Calzones
Address: 108 W. Green St., Ithaca
Phone: (607) 277-7772
Cool Features: DP Dough, a favorite late-night snack for IC students, offers nearly fifty varieties of calzones.
Price: $6 and under per person
Hours: Monday-Tuesday 4 p.m.-2 a.m., Thursday 4 p.m.-3 a.m., Friday-Saturday 11 a.m.-4 a.m., Sunday 11 a.m.-2 a.m.

Franco's Italian Restaurant
Food: Italian, pizza
Address: 825 Danby Road, Ithaca
Phone: (607) 277-6666
Price: $15 and under per person
Hours: Sunday-Thursday 11 a.m.-9 p.m., Friday-Saturday 11 a.m.-10 p.m.

Friendly's
Food: American, ice cream
Address: 40 Catherwood Rd., Ithaca
Phone: (607) 257-2361
Price: $10 and under per person
Hours: Monday-Saturday 9 a.m.-9 p.m., Sunday 11 a.m.-5 p.m.

Gino's New York Pizzeria
Food: Italian, pizza
Address: 106 N. Aurora St., Ithaca
Phone: (607) 277-2777
Price: $5 and under per person
Hours: Sunday-Wednesday 11 a.m.-1 a.m., Friday-Saturday 11 a.m.-3 a.m.

Ithaca Bakery
Food: Baked goods
Address: 400 N. Meadow St., Ithaca
Phone: (607) 273-7110
Price: $5 and under per person
Hours: Monday-Sunday 6 a.m.-8 p.m.

Ithaca Diner
Food: American, breakfast
Adress: 116 W. State St., Ithaca
Phone: (607) 272-6009
Price: $10 and under per person
Hours: 24 hours a day

Jade Garden
Food: Chinese
Address: 113 N. Aurora St., Ithaca
Phone: (607) 272-8880
Price: $10 and under per person
Hours: Monday-Sunday 11 a.m.-11 p.m.

John Thomas Steakhouse
Food: Steak
Address: 1152 Darby Rd., Ithaca
Phone: (607) 273-3464
Fax: (607) 237-4747
Price: $25 and under per person
Hours: Monday-Sunday 5:30 p.m.-11 p.m.

King Buffet
Food: Chinese
Address: 734 S. Meadows St., Ithaca
Phone: (607) 256-3388
Fax: (607) 256-0821
Price: $15 and under per person
Hours: Monday-Sunday 11 a.m.-10 p.m.

Lost Dog Café
Food: Eclectic, coffeshop
Address: 106-112 S. Cayuga St., Ithaca
Phone: (607) 277-9143
Price: $15 and under
Hours: Tuesday-Friday 11:30 a.m.-2:30 p.m., 5 p.m.-10 p.m., Saturday 11:30 a.m.-10 p.m., Sunday 11:30 a.m.-9 p.m., lounge open Monday 6 p.m.-midnight, Thursday-Saturday 6 p.m.-1 a.m.

Madeline's
Food: French, Asian
Address: The Commons, 215 E. State St., Ithaca
Phone: (607) 277-2253
Price: $20 and under per person
Hours: Sunday-Thursday 5 p.m.-10 p.m., Friday-Saturday 5 p.m.-11 p.m.

Mahogany Grill
Food: American
Address: 114 N. Aurora St., Ithaca
Phone: (607) 272-1438
Price: $25 and under per person
Hours: Sunday-Thursday 11 a.m.-10 p.m., Friday-Saturday 11 a.m.-11 p.m.

Mano's Diner
Food: American Cuisine
Address: 357 Elmira Rd., Ithaca
Phone: (607) 273-9522
Price: $20 and under per person
Hours: 24 hours a day

Maxie's Supper Club & Oyster Bar
Food: Cajun, seafood
Address: 635 W. State St., Ithaca
Phone: (607) 272-4136
Fax: (607) 253-0486
Cool Features: live music, raw oyster bar half-price 4

Maxie's (*Continued...*)
p.m-6 p.m., late-night bites $2.50 two hours before close
Price: $20 and under per person
Hours: Sunday-Thursday 4 p.m.-midnight, Friday-Saturday 4 p.m.-1 a.m.

Moosewood Restaurant
Food: Vegetarian
Address: Dewitt Mall, 215 N. Cayuga St., Ithaca
Phone: (607) 273-9610
Cool Features: Moosewood is nationally-known for their vegetarian food, and the menu changes daily. For those who still want some meat with their dinner, Moosewood offers fish as well.
Price: $15 and under per person
Hours: lunch Monday-Saturday 11:30 a.m.-3 p.m., dinner Sunday-Thursday 5:30 p.m.-8:30 p.m., Friday-Saturday 5:30 p.m.-9 p.m.

Napoli's Pizzaria
Food: Pizza, subs
Address: 335 E. State St., Ithaca
Phone: (607) 272-3232
Price: $10 and under per person
Hours: Sunday-Thursday 11 a.m.-1 a.m., Friday-Saturday 11 a.m.-2 a.m.

Pangea
Food: Eclectic
Address: 130 Third St.,
Ithaca
Phone: (607) 273-8515
Price: $20 and under per
person
Hours: Wednesday-Monday
5:30 p.m.-10 p.m.

Purity Ice Cream
Food: Ice cream
Address: 700 Cascadilla St.,
Ithaca
Phone: (607) 272-1545
Price: $5 and under per
person
Hours: Sunday-Thursday 11
a.m.-9 p.m., Friday-Saturday
11 a.m.-11 p.m.

Ragmann's
Food: Gourmet sandwiches
Address: 108 N. Aurora St.,
Ithaca
Phone: (607) 273-5236
Price: $10 and under per
person
Hours: Monday-Sunday
11:30 a.m.-9 p.m.

Simeon's on The Commons
Food: American
Address: The Commons, 224
E. State St., Ithaca
Phone: (607) 272-2212
Cool Features: outdoor café,
Price: $25 and under per
person
Hours: Monday-Sunday 11
a.m.-midnight

Souvlaki House
Food: Greek
Address: 315 Eddy St.,
Ithaca
Phone: (607) 273-1650
Price: $10 and under per
person
Hours: Monday-Sunday 11
a.m.-11 p.m.

The Station
Food: American
Address: 806 W. Buffalo St.,
Ithaca
Phone: (607) 272-2609
Price: $20 and under per
person
Hours: Tuesday-Friday 4
p.m.-9 p.m., Saturday 4 p.m.-
9:30 p.m., Sunday 12 p.m.-8
p.m.

**Stella's Kitchen and
Cocktails**
Food: Gourmet American,
coffeshop
Address: 403 College Ave.,
Ithaca
Phone: (607) 277-1490
Fax: (607) 277-1519
Price: $15 and under per
person
Hours: restaurant Monday-
Sunday 11 a.m.-12 a.m.,
coffeeshop Monday-Sunday
7 pm.-1 a.m.

Taste of Thai
Food: Thai
Address: The Commons, 216 State St., Ithaca
Phone: (607) 256-5487
Fax: (607) 256-8051
Price: $15 and under per person
Hours: Monday-Sunday 11:30 a.m.-2:30 p.m. and 5 p.m.-10 p.m.

Thai Cuisine
Food: Thai
Address: 501 S. Meadow St., Ithaca
Phone: (607) 273-2031
Price: $15 and under per person
Hours: Sunday-Thursday 5 p.m.-9:30 p.m., Sunday brunch 11:30 a.m.-2 p.m., Friday-Saturday 5 p.m.-10 p.m., Saturday lunch 11:30 a.m.-2:30 p.m., Closed Tuesday.

Viva Taqueria/Cantina
Food: Mexican
Address: 101/103 N. Aurora St., Ithaca
Phone: (607) 277-1752
Price: $10 and under per person
Hours: Monday-Sunday 11 a.m.-10 p.m.

Wegmans Market Cafe
Food: American, Chinese, vegetarian, deli
Address: 800 S. Meadow St., Ithaca
Phone: (607) 277-1775
Fax: (607) 274-8640
Price: $7 and under per person
Hours: Monday-Sunday 8 a.m.-9 p.m.

Willow
Food: American
Address: 202 E. Falls St., Ithaca
Phone: (607) 272-0656
Price: $20 and under per person
Hours: Tuesday-Saturday 5 p.m.-10 p.m.

Wings Over Ithaca
Food: Wings
Address: E. Hill Plaza, Ithaca
Phone: (607) 256-9464
Cool Features: tasty boneless chicken wings
Price: $7 and under per person
Hours: Monday 4 p.m.-1 a.m., Sunday, Tuesday, and Wednesday 11 a.m.-1 a.m., Thursday-Saturday 11 a.m.-3 a.m.

Student Favorites:
The Boatyard Grill
Wings Over Ithaca
Viva Taqueria/Cantina

24-Hour Eating:
Mano's
Ithaca Diner

Closest Grocery Stores:
Wegmans
800 S. Meadow St.
Ithaca
(607) 277-5800
Open 24 hours

Tops Friendly Markets
710 S. Meadow St.
Ithaca
(607) 275-8041
Open 24 hours

Best Pizza:
Gino's New York Pizzeria

Best Chinese:
Jade Garden

Best Breakfast:
Ithaca Bakery

Best Wings:
Wings Over Ithaca

Best Healthy:
Moosewood Restaurant

Best Place to Take Your Parents:
The Boatyard Grill

Did You Know?

Fun Facts
Ithaca has **more restaurants** per capita than any other place in the country.

• Organic Style named Ithaca **the healthiest city** in the Northeast.

• The **first ice cream sundae** was supposedly made in Ithaca.

Students Speak Out On...
Off-Campus Dining

"The food in Ithaca is generally very good, as long as you remember that people in the Northeast do not know how to make Mexican food! There are a ton of places to eat in Ithaca and Collegetown, and most of them deliver as well."

Q "**There are a ton of great restaurants in Ithaca,** and lots of different options. Taste of Thai downtown is great if you like Asian food, The Boatyard Grill is good for a nicer, but still casual meal, and the Souvlaki House in Collegetown is great if you want a big Italian/Greek meal for not too much money."

Q "The Chinese buffet on Route 13 is good. If you want something at five o'clock in the morning, **there are a few 24-hour diners that are kind of fun.** Oh yeah, and D.P. Dough is great. And since I'm on the topic of delivery, Jade Garden is the best delivery Chinese place."

Q "**Some of my favorites:** Taste of Thai, Collegetown Bagels, Wings over Ithaca, Stella's."

Q "Very good, but some are overpriced. **The Moosewood is great for vegetarians and omnivores alike**, and the Mahogany Grill is a great place to take your parents when they come to visit."

Q "The only times I eat out are when my parents come to visit, but **there are a lot of places in the Commons,** and around the area."

Q "There are tons of restaurants off campus. **The best pizza in town is Gino's on the Commons.** The 'fancier setting' meal is at the Boatyard Grill. The best homemade ice cream in town is at Purity Ice Cream. The best bakery is, hands down, Ithaca Bakery, which also owns the Collegetown Bagels locations. There are at least four Chinese places, which all deliver. Ithaca has three Friendly's and just got an Applebee's and a Chili's. Collegetown and the Commons are the best places to find a meal, if you're unsure about what to eat."

Q "Depending on what you're looking for there are hundreds of restaurant options in Ithaca and the surrounding towns. Students and parents love the Boatyard Grill because it's delicious, and the atmosphere and service are superb. **Napoli's is a great place for excellent pizza and wings at a low cost**, and the nearby Chinese King Buffet boasts a seventy-five foot buffet line with American and Chinese choices including snow crab legs every night."

Q "**Ithaca actually has a great variety of restaurants**, with anything from Thai to Mexican to Indian food. Personally, my favorite is Thai food (Taste of Thai and Thai Cuisine). It's excellent here. We also have the typical restaurants such as Applebees, Chili's, Friendly's, and Mano's."

Q "**There are many restaurants off campus in the Commons that are very good**, and you can access them even without a car because the bus service that runs down to the Commons is pretty cheap."

Q "It's very good, but hard to find something to fit a diverse group of tastes. **I recommend the Lost Dog Café highly**, as well as Simeon's if you aren't in a hurry."

Q "Oh my goodness. So many places to eat. **I'll never ever be able to try everything.** They have the typical chains like Applebees, Friendly's, and I believe Chili's is opening up sometime in the near future."

Q There are hundreds of privately owned places that are amazing. **My friends and I use a website, http://www.14850.com, to scope out the restaurants** when we want to try something new. They give categories and reviews on each one and often times they provide the restaurant's website to see a sample menu."

Q "Ithaca has more restaurants per capita than any other city around. **You can find any type of food you want, at any price level,** not to mention the wealth of fast food and convenience joints."

Q "The restaurants off campus have a ton of character and delicious food. **They are easy to drive to and comfortable to dine in.** For a fancy occasion and the best steak in town, go to John Thomas. For a lively atmosphere with terrific food, go to the Boatyard. For a quirky setting and varied dishes, go to the Lost Dog Café. There is also a great selection of ethnic food places including Indian, Thai, Italian, and Middle Eastern. And there are always the good old fashioned bars and bagel joints that are so prevalent in college towns."

Q "Whenever my family comes to visit we go out to eat at one of Ithaca's fine restaurants. **I enjoyed the Station, where we got to eat in a train**. The Boatyard Grill is pretty good too. Make sure you stop by the Ithaca Bakery for breakfast."

Q "If I'm going out, there's a really good healthy Mexican restaurant right when you get to the Commons downtown. As far as ordering in, **D.P. Dough is a staple among college students**; they have great calzones."

Q **"Benchwarmers has great bar food,** cute little Ithaca restaurants like Simeon's and Viva Taquería offer Ithaca-esque small town dining. Collegetown Bagels has some of the coolest little sandwiches and breakfast options ever."

The College Prowler Take On...
Off-Campus Dining

Feel like a hamburger? Chinese? Thai? Pizza? Vegetarian? Whatever a person's tastes, Ithaca has it covered. With countless options, at times making a choice can be difficult. For a quick bite, Route 13 offers just about every fast-food chain around, and the Commons, Collegetown, and downtown areas offer sandwich shops and delis, cafés, fine dining, bars, and plenty of take-out and delivery. Try Taste of Thai, the Lost Dog, and Stella's. For all of those dates with that special someone, Ithaca offers many options to make that night perfect. The Boatyard Grill, located next to the lake, offers surf and turf. The world famous Moosewood Restaurant calls Ithaca home, and with its delicious vegetarian specialties, even a steak lover will find something tasty.

Living in the city with most restaurants per capita definitely has its perks. It's nice to escape campus food and to discover some of the tastes that make Ithaca unique. Grab some friends and head to the Commons or Collegetown, and you're met with a wealth of dining pleasures. When you're in the mood for a study break at 2 a.m., don't hesitate to order a pizza or calzone, because most places deliver at least that late.

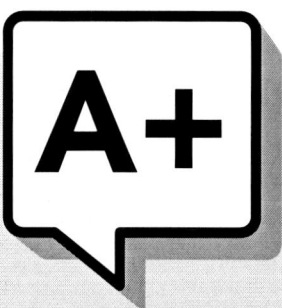

The College Prowler™ Grade on

Off-Campus Dining: A+

A high off-campus dining grade implies that off-campus restaurants are affordable, accessible, and worth visiting. Other factors include the variety of cuisine and the availability of alternative options (vegetarian, vegan, Kosher, etc.).

On-Campus Housing

The Lowdown On...
On-Campus Housing

Room Types:

Single: Student lives by him or herself

Double: Student lives with one other person

Triple: Student lives with two other people

Suite: Students share a living area with bedrooms adjacent. Some suites have private bathrooms.

Apartments are located on campus and can accommodate from two to six people. The apartments include private bathrooms, a kitchen and a living area.

Best Dorms:

College Circle Apartments

Garden Apartments

Upper Quads (Holmes, Talcott, Rowland, Hilliard, Hood)

Emerson

Worst Dorms:

Boothroyd

Lower Quads (Eastman, Lyon, Clarke, Bogart, Landon)

Dormitories

Bogart

Floors: 3 + basement

Total Occupancy: 128

Bathrooms: Shared by floor

Co-Ed: Yes

Percentage of Men/ Women: 50%/50%

Percentage of First-Year Students: 68%

Room Types: Singles, doubles

Special Features: Vending machines, microwaves, lounges, laundry facilities, public kitchens

Boothroyd

Floors: 2

Total Occupancy: 100

Bathrooms: Shared by floor

Co-Ed: Yes

Percentage of Men/ Women: 50%/50%

Percentage of First-Year Students: 100%

Room Types: Singles, doubles

Special Features: Elevators, vending machines, microwaves, lounges, laundry facilities, public kitchens. Boothroyd is part of the First-Year Program.

Clarke

Floors: 3

Total Occupancy: 112

Bathrooms: Shared by floor

Co-Ed: Yes

Percentage of Men/ Women: 50%/50%

Percentage of First-Year Students: 83%

Room Types: Singles, doubles

Special Features: Vending machines, microwaves, lounges, laundry facilities, public kitchens

Eastman

Floors: 3

Total Occupancy: 110

Bathrooms: Shared by floor

Co-Ed: Yes

Percentage of Men/ Women: 31%/69%

Percentage of First-Year Students: 76%

Room Types: Singles, doubles

Special Features: Vending machines, microwaves, lounges, laundry facilities, public kitchens

College Circle Apartments

Floors: Varies by building

Total Occupancy: 690

Eastman (*Continued...*)

Bathrooms: Private

Co-Ed: Yes

Percentage of Men/ Women: 42%/58%

Percentage of First-Year Students: 7%

Room Types: 2, 3, 4, 5, or 6-person apartments

Special Features: Private kitchens, living areas

East Tower

Floors: 13

Total Occupancy: 323

Bathrooms: Shared by floor

Co-Ed: Yes

Percentage of Men/ Women: 40%/60%

Percentage of First-Year Students: 83%

Room Types: Single, double

Special Features: Non-smoking, elevators, vending machines, public kitchen, television lounge, study lounges, laundry facilities

Emerson

Floors: 3

Total Occupancy: 283

Bathrooms: Private

Co-Ed: Yes, by door

Percentage of Men/

Emerson (*Continued...*)

Women: 49%/51%

Percentage of First-Year Students: 47%

Room Types: Double, triple

Special Features: First floor is non-smoking, air-conditioning, elevators, vending machines, public kitchen, television lounge, study lounges, laundry facilities

Garden Apartments

Floors: Varies by building

Total Occupancy: 408

Bathrooms: Private

Co-Ed: Yes, by door

Percentage of Men/ Women: 33%/67%

Percentage of First-Year Students: 10%

Room Types: 2, 4, or 6-person apartments

Special Features: Private kitchens, living areas

Hilliard

Floors: 3

Total Occupancy: 115

Bathrooms: Shared by floor

Co-Ed: Yes

Percentage of Men/ Women: 35%/65%

Hilliard (*Continued...*)

Percentage of First-Year Students: 55%

Room Types: Singles, doubles

Special Features: Vending machines, microwaves, lounges, laundry facilities, public kitchens

Holmes

Floors: 3

Total Occupancy: 109

Bathrooms: Shared by floor

Co-Ed: Yes

Percentage of Men/ Women: 45%/55%

Percentage of First-Year Students: 16%

Room Types: Singles, doubles

Special Features: Vending machines, microwaves, lounges, laundry facilities, public kitchens

Hood

Floors: 3

Total Occupancy: 115

Bathrooms: Shared by floor

Co-Ed: Yes

Percentage of Men/ Women: 48%/52%

Percentage of First-Year Students: 48%

Hood (*Continued...*)

Room Types: Singles, doubles

Special Features: Vending machines, microwaves, lounges, laundry facilities, public kitchens

Landon

Floors: 3 + basement

Total Occupancy: 131

Bathrooms: Shared by floor

Co-Ed: Yes

Percentage of Men/ Women: 47%/53%

Percentage of First-Year Students: 71%

Room Types: Singles, doubles

Special Features: Vending machines, microwaves, lounges, laundry facilities, public kitchens. The basement of Landon houses the honors program of the School of Humanities and Sciences.

Lyon

Floors: 3 + basement

Total Occupancy:

Bathrooms: Shared by floor

Co-Ed: Yes

Percentage of Men/ Women: 35%/65%

Lyon *(Continued...)*

Percentage of First-Year Students: 77%

Room Types: Singles, doubles

Special Features: Vending machines, microwaves, lounges, laundry facilities, public kitchens

Rowland

Floors: 3 + basement

Total Occupancy: 125

Bathrooms: Shared by floor

Co-Ed: Yes

Percentage of Men/ Women: 30%/70%

Percentage of First-Year Students: 100%

Room Types: Singles, doubles

Special Features: Vending machines, microwaves, lounges, laundry facilities, public kitchens. Rowland is part of the First-Year Program.

Tallcott

Floors: 3

Total Occupancy: 111

Bathrooms: Shared by floor

Co-Ed: Yes

Percentage of Men/ Women: 34%/66%

Tallcott *(Continued...)*

Percentage of First-Year Students: 100%

Room Types: Singles, doubles

Special Features: Vending machines, microwaves, lounges, laundry facilities, public kitchens. Tallcott is part of the First-Year Program.

Terrace 1

Floors: 3

Total Occupancy: 52

Bathrooms: Shared by floor

Co-Ed: No

Percentage of Men/ Women: 0%/100%

Percentage of First-Year Students: 34%

Room Types: Singles, Doubles, Suites

Special Features: Vending machines, microwaves, lounges, laundry facilities, public kitchens, dumbwaiters

Terrace 2

Floors: 3

Total Occupancy: 61

Bathrooms: Shared by floor

Co-Ed: Yes

Percentage of Men/ Women: 30%/70%

Terrace 2 (*Continued...*)

Percentage of First-Year Students: 67%

Room Types: Singles, doubles, suites, triples

Special Features: Vending machines, microwaves, lounges, laundry facilities, public kitchens, dumbwaiters

Terrace 3

Floors: 3

Total Occupancy: 97

Bathrooms: Shared by floor

Co-Ed: Yes, by door

Percentage of Men/Women: 45%/55%

Percentage of First-Year Students: 24%

Room Types: Singles, doubles, suites, triples

Special Features: Vending machines, microwaves, lounges, laundry facilities, public kitchens, dumbwaiters. Terrace 2 is also the Housing Offering Multicultural Experience (H.O.M.E.) Program.

Terrace 4

Floors: 3

Total Occupancy: 72

Bathrooms: Shared by floor

Co-Ed: Yes, by door

Percentage of Men: 43%

Terrace 4 (*Continued...*)

Women: 57%

Percentage of First-Year Students: 19%

Room Types: Singles, doubles, suites, triples

Special Features: Vending machines, microwaves, lounges, laundry facilities, public kitchens, dumbwaiters

Terrace 5

Floors: 3

Total Occupancy: 58

Bathrooms: Shared by floor

Co-Ed: Yes

Percentage of Men/Women: 38%/62%

Percentage of First-Year Students: 36%

Room Types: Singles, doubles, suites, triples

Special Features: Vending machines, microwaves, lounges, laundry facilities, public kitchens, dumbwaiters, Quiet Study Program.

Terrace 6

Floors: 3

Total Occupancy: 106

Bathrooms: Shared by floor

Co-Ed: Yes

Percentage of Men/Women: 49%/51%

Terrace 6 (*Continued...*)

Percentage of First-Year Students: 34%

Room Types: Singles, doubles, suites, triples

Special Features: Vending machines, microwaves, lounges, laundry facilities, public kitchens, dumbwaiters

Terrace 7

Floors: 3

Total Occupancy: 112

Bathrooms: Shared by floor

Co-Ed: Yes

Percentage of Men/ Women: 36%/64%

Percentage of First-Year Students: 33%

Room Types: Singles, doubles, suites, triples

Special Features: Vending machines, microwaves, lounges, laundry facilities, public kitchens, dumbwaiters

Terrace 8

Floors: 3

Total Occupancy: 84

Bathrooms: Shared by floor

Co-Ed: Yes, by door

Percentage of Men/ Women: 36%/64%

Percentage of First-Year Students: 27%

Terrace 8 (*Continued...*)

Room Types: Singles, doubles, suites, triples

Special Features: Vending Machines, microwaves, lounges, laundry facilities, public kitchens, dumbwaiters

Terrace 9

Floors: 3

Total Occupancy: 95

Bathrooms: Shared by floor

Co-Ed: Yes

Percentage of Men/ Women: 50%/50%

Percentage of First-Year Students: 23%

Room Types: Singles, doubles, suites, triples

Special Features: Vending machines, microwaves, lounges, laundry facilities, public kitchens, dumbwaiters

Terrace 10

Floors: 3

Total Occupancy: 103

Bathrooms: Shared by floor

Co-Ed: Yes

Percentage of Men/ Women: 47%/53%

Percentage of First-Year Students: 47%

Room Types: Singles, doubles, suites, triples

Terrace 10 (*Cont'd...*)

Special Features: Vending machines, microwaves, lounges, laundry facilities, public kitchens, dumbwaiters

Terrace 11

Floors: 3

Total Occupancy: 102

Bathrooms: Shared by floor

Co-Ed: Yes, by door

Percentage of Men/ Women: 45%/55%

Percentage of First-Year Students: 41%

Room Types: Singles, doubles, triples

Special Features: Vending machines, microwaves, lounges, laundry facilities, public kitchens, dumbwaiters

Terrace 12

Floors: 3

Total Occupancy: 95

Bathrooms: Shared by Floor

Co-Ed: Yes

Percentage of Men/ Women: 80%/20%

Percentage of First-Year Students: 63%

Room Types: Singles, doubles, triples

Special Features: Vending machines,microwaves

West Tower

Floors: 13

Total Occupancy: 322

Bathrooms: Shared by floor

Co-Ed: Yes

Percentage of Men/ Women: 40%/60%

Percentage of First-Year Students: 70%

Room Types: Single, double

Special Features: Non-smoking, elevators, vending machines, public kitchen, television lounge, study lounges, laundry facilities

Number of Dormitory Residents:

Undergrads on Campus: 70%

Number of Dormitories:

26

Number of University-Owned Apartments:

26 apartment buildings, 1098 beds

Bed Type:

Twin extra long (39"x80"), bunk and loft requests can be made once you arrive on campus

Available for Rent

Through a company hired by the school, students can rent Microfridges, which are a microwave and refrigerator combination, and mini refrigerators. Microfridges are popular among students because student-brought microwaves are not permitted in dorm rooms.

Cleaning Service?

Public areas, such as bathrooms shared by a floor, are cleaned each weekday.

You Get

Bed, desk and chair, dresser, closet, window coverings, cable TV jack, Ethernet internet connection, free campus and local phone calls

Also Available

The first floor of Emerson, Garden Apartments 25 and 26, some College Circle Apartments, Terraces 4, 6, 7, 9 and 10, Hood, Tallcott, Rowland, Boothroyd, Landon, Bogart, Clarke, and Eastman are all non-smoking dorms.

- Boothroyd, Rowland, and Tallcott house the First-Year Program.
- Hood is substance-free housing.
- Terrace 2 offers the Housing Offering a Multicultural Experience (H.O.M.E.) program.
- Professional fraternities may live in Terraces 4, 8, 9, and 12.

Did You Know?

Most freshmen who decide to live in the First Year Program find that it is a very rewarding experience because **they live with all freshmen,** and programs are designed to ease the transition into college.

• After students' freshmen year, they can apply to live in a **Garden or College Circle Apartment,** which means the meal plan is no longer required. This saves a lot of money, even when food has to be bought at the grocery store.

"The dorms aren't too bad. The Lower Quads are sketchy, the Towers are loud, the Terraces and Circles are a long walk from the academic buildings. Personally, I like the Gardens and Upper Quads the best."

Q "I like all the dorms. The best, of course, are the Circle Apartments. They rock. I also like the Upper Quads. **The Terraces are removed but nice.**"

Q "The dorms are small, but there are a lot of them. Live in the Terraces if you want to have a pretty view and a long walk to class. **Live in the Circles if you want to believe you're not on campus,** and want a really long walk, or a heck of a time finding a parking spot. The Upper Quads are really convenient, but can get rowdy."

Q "From what I've seen, **the dorms are all pretty nice**. The rooms in Boothroyd are pretty small, though, and I'd say avoid the Terraces unless you want to have to hike there and back up numerous amounts of stairs to go from classes back to your room."

Q "Freshman dorms are typical of many colleges. The dorms in the terraces are the biggest, but the farthest away from everything. Dorms in the Upper Quad area are the newest and cleanest, and much closer than Terraces. Dorms in the Towers are worst. J**uniors and seniors can live in on-campus apartments,** which are beautiful and fully furnished."

Q "**Dorms are functional, but ugly**. I can't say which dorms to avoid because some are in better locations than others for certain buildings. The Quads are closest to the Fitness Center, and the Towers are closer to the library, the music building, and the best dining hall. The nicest ones are the Terraces and Emerson, although they're farther away from everything. Avoid the Garden Apartments and go for a Circle Apartment. Circles are so nice."

Q "Avoid the Towers, unless you like living in 14-story buildings with slow, if working, elevators with all of your closest freshman friends. **The Terraces are nice**, but are like their own enclave because they are up the hill from the other dorms. The newly acquired Circles apartments, which used to be off-campus housing, are really far away from campus. It takes about a twenty to thirty minute walk to get to the farthest academic building, and that's without snow.

Q "The Quads are convenient because they're in the center of everything. If you can abide by the rules, Hood, the substance-free dorm, was just renovated in 2001, and is beautiful. **Emerson is the only dorm with air-conditioning.** And Boothroyd, part of the freshman housing program, has double rooms that were originally supposed to be singles, so they are very cramped."

Q "The residence halls are very old fashioned. Some are definitely better than others. **I suggest, for any incoming freshman, to live in the First Year Program.** It's a great way to meet people and it's more nurturing. They have programs geared towards first year students to make the transition to college easier."

Q "I liked freshman housing for the experience because it was very easy to meet people. We had an open door policy, and it was comforting to know all the people in your building. **I wouldn't recommend Towers to upperclassmen** because it's mainly freshmen, and the elevators are your main method of getting to your floor."

Q "Hands down, the best dorms to live in as a freshman are the Towers. In addition to being close to the best dining hall on campus, **they each have their own mailroom,** they are less than ten minutes from anywhere on campus (except for the Circle Apartments), and the Towers concourse is also home to BJ's, a convenience store that is open until 1 a.m."

Q "Although Emerson has private bathrooms, **you get used to having to walk down the hall in a towel.** The Quads are close to Campus Center and some of the academic buildings, but they are generally not worth your while unless you have a single."

Q "I love my dorm room. Last year I lived in a First Year Program dorm and it was the most amazing experience of my life. I miss it a lot, but my dorm room now is practically identical, and I am content. There are basically three basic tradition type dorms. The Quads, which are what I have always lived in, are simple but really nice. They renovate one every summer. **I have a good amount of shelves** and the amount of space is perfect."

Q **"The Towers can get loud and crowded,** but people who live there often say it's a great time and that they really bond with their floor. Lastly, there are the Terraces. They are a fun place to live and don't really give off as much of the dorm room feel, but they are the furthest away, which still isn't too far. Also there are apartments, the Gardens and the Circles."

Q "**The dorms are great.** They are homey and you can make them your own. It is also the perfect way to meet new people. Activities are always going on and there is a real sense of community in them. I prefer the Quad dorms because they are close to everything and I like the general set-up."

Q "I currently live in Boothroyd Hall, the smallest dorm on campus. All the other dorms are huge compared to mine. Living here wasn't bad at all this year. It's a little tight for space, but it's still bigger than most other college dorms I looked at. The only thing I would like is my own bathroom; **communal bathrooms get pretty gross."**

Q "The dorms are alright, nothing special. Living in the First Year Program dorms (Rowland, Tallcott and Boothroyd, though Boothroyd is crappy and small) is a really great way to make friends and makes freshmen year enjoyable. Personally, the Upper Quads are usually a safe bet if you have to live in the dorms. Lower Quads are pretty bad from what I've seen. **The Circle Apartments are really nice, but they're mostly for upperclassmen,** and it's better if you have a car because they're not very close."

Q **"Avoid Clarke,** but above all, avoid the Towers."

Q "The Circles and Gardens are obviously the nicest, with more space, a kitchen and family room. The on-campus housing is pretty tight (small space), but I would recommend living in the dorms at some point just to make connections on campus. **I would recommend the Towers with a view of the lake on one of the higher floors.** I faced the lake freshman year on the eighth floor and it was the most gorgeous view. I miss that so much now!"

The College Prowler Take On...
On-Campus Housing

IC is a residential college, which means that all students, except for seniors, are expected to live on campus. But with the recent addition of the College Circle Apartments, many students choose to stay on campus for four years. In the Circles and in the Garden Apartments, students are given the option of living more independently because they are not required to purchase a meal plan. Boothroyd Hall, one of the upper quads and part of the First Year Program, is the worst dorm on campus. IC built the dorm rooms as singles, but then converted them into freshmen doubles. The rooms are very tiny (the beds need to be lofted just to fit a dresser in the room), but the size of the rooms brings a unique bond to the residents of "The Boot." The Towers are known for being loud, but when it's cold, it's nice to not have to venture outside to go to a dining hall. The Terraces are far from the center of campus, and it can be a pain to walk up and down all the stairs. Emerson Hall has private bathrooms, but you can get used to sharing one with your floormates in the other halls.

IC offers many housing options, and most students are generally happy with where they live. The special housing dorms can be very beneficial for those who are interested. Skilled Resident Assistants are required to design informational programs for their residents, and the RAs are there when their residents get locked out, are confused about how to register for classes, or just need someone to listen. The residents of most dorms form tight communities, and some dorms even form teams for intramural sports.

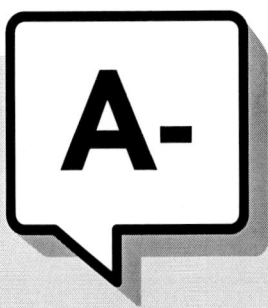

The College Prowler™ Grade on

Campus Housing: A-

A high Campus Housing grade indicates that dorms are clean, well-maintained, and spacious. Other determining factors include variety of dorms, proximity to classes, and social atmosphere.

Off-Campus Housing

The Lowdown On...
Off-Campus Housing

Undergrads in Off-Campus Housing:
30%

Best Time to Look for a Place:
10 or 11 months in advance—September or October for the following school year

Average Rent:
Most students rent houses or apartments with their friends. Landlords usually charge anywhere between $350-$450 per person/month.

Popular Areas:
Coddington
Hillview
Kendall
Pennsylvania

Students Speak Out On...
Off-Campus Housing

"Housing off campus after freshman year is hard to attain for many people. I don't think it's worth it. I'd rather be on campus, close to everything."

Q "I think the main problem with living off-campus is driving in bad weather and **finding a parking spot.**"

Q "They don't let very many people live off campus until their senior year. It's worth it for the money because **Ithaca is so expensive**, and you save at least a couple thousand dollars in room and board. You might want to have a car, or live with someone who has one, because the bus system is kind of expensive and the walk up the hill to school is a big one. Keep in mind, it's hard to find a parking spot if you do have a car."

Q "You can't move off-campus until senior year. **Apartments seem to be available**, but most students sign leases in September or October for the following academic year."

Q "**It's really hard to get a spot off campus unless you're a senior** or you have a really good lottery number, which is based on the number of credits you have and your class standing. I'd say it's worth it if a) you have a car that can handle snow and hills, b) you have an off-campus job or internship, and/or c) you really like to party."

Q "They just acquired the Circles Apartments, so almost no one except for seniors get off-campus allowances. **I have found it more convenient to stay on campus**, even as a senior, so I did not have the hassle of driving to class in bad weather, or being too isolated from campus."

Q "I don't particularly like any of the houses off campus. To me, **they seem run down and very ugly.** I would prefer to live in the Circle Apartments."

Q "It is much easier to get off-campus housing after your sophomore year. The college provides a lot of housing on campus, though. **There are many new apartments available for upperclassman,** and if you move off campus, it isn't too hard to get a place to live."

Q "Because Ithaca College is a 'residential college,' there is little chance of living off campus until your junior year, and you are not assured a spot off campus until your senior year. Living off campus will save you a ton of money, as Ithaca College charges almost $10,000 a year to live on campus, but if you don't have a car, **commuting will be a huge hassle.**"

Q "Well, its convenient in the sense that it's not too far away and in **a lot of places you can even deal with not having a car,** but Ithaca is a residence based school, and anyone who isn't a senior who wants to live off campus needs to get permission. I don't know how hard it is. The only reason I think I will want to live off campus in the future is to learn how to do the whole house thing."

Q "**It saved me about $3,500 between food and housing.** And I'm right across from the back entrance to the college, which is nice. It's closer than the Terraces."

The College Prowler Take On...
Off-Campus Housing

Since IC is a residential college, unless you're a senior you must go through an application process to be granted off-campus status. All freshmen must live on campus, and seniors are automatically given the ability to move off campus if they desire. Because of hassles with parking on campus, a lot of students find it easier to live close enough to walk. Off-campus students also have more problems with paying bills and not being on the campus internet network. Most students sign leases in September or October for the next fall, and it's advised to read leases carefully.

There are many different housing options available off campus for students. From one-room efficiencies to houses you can rent with your ten closest friends, if you want to live off campus there is housing available to suit your needs. With the recent addition of the College Circle Apartments, more students are finding that it is just easier to remain on campus all four years. Still, with on-campus housing ranging from anywhere between $5,000 to $7,000 per year, many students opt to find alternative, money-saving options.

The College Prowler™ Grade on
Off-Campus
Housing: B+

A high grade in Off-Campus Housing indicates that apartments are of high quality, close to campus, affordable, and easy to secure.

Diversity

The Lowdown On...
Diversity

American Indian:
0.35%

Asian or Pacific Islander:
2.7%

African American:
2.4%

Hispanic:
2.9%

White:
87%

International:
3.3%

Unknown:
1%

Out-of-State:
51.3%

Political Activity

The city of Ithaca is known as one of the most liberal cities in the country, but all aspects of the political spectrum are visible in student organizations. Green party candidate Ralph Nader, and conservative activist Bay Buchanan both spoke on campus in 2002. Clubs on campus include IC Democrats, Ithaca College Republicans, and Students for a Just Peace. Besides bringing speakers to campus, the groups often host debates, voter registration drives, and forums. In the midst of the United States going to war with Iraq, protests could be seen around campus almost daily.

Gay Tolerance

Every April, the college celebrates "Gaypril," a month long event that strives to make the public more tolerant and increase awareness of homosexual students. During this month the Rainbow Pride flag flies on a flagpole in the center of campus. The college has a Center for Lesbian, Gay, Bisexual, Transgender, Education, Outreach, and Services which strives to make the campus a better environment for LGBT people. Many professors have "Safe Place" signs on their doors. The purpose of these signs is to make LGBT students feel more comfortable discussing issues concerning their sexuality. Groups such as BIGAYLA and Created Equal have a presence on campus. Many speakers and movies are sponsored by these groups.

Most Popular Religions

Muller Chapel holds services for Catholic, Jewish and Protestant faiths. There's a multitude of churches off campus as well that students attend. Students for Christ and Chi Alpha also have visible roles on campus.

Economic Status

Most students on campus can be classified as middle to upper-middle class, but like any place, you find a wide variety of backgrounds. You will see students parking their Mercedes SUVs next to used cars that have seen better days.

Minority Clubs

Groups such as the African Latino Society and Asian Culture Club sponsor events and bring speakers to campus to try to increase awareness about other races and cultures.

Students Speak Out On...
Diversity

"We have a lot of different countries represented, I suppose, but I don't really learn too much about the world from having them here. There is a rich community around us; people just have to open their eyes to it."

Q "I don't think campus is diverse enough, but the college is making an effort to make it more diverse."

Q "There are a good number of international students, but the ethnic groups definitely tend to run in the same circles."

Q "It's very, very Caucasian and upper-middle class."

Q "The college is trying to improve diversity, but the numbers don't seem to be changing from year to year. The college also stresses diversity of skin color over other types of diversity, which I think is detrimental to the student body."

Q "IC markets and advertises as if it's super diverse, but it isn't. The only difference between the diversity here and that of my white suburban high school is IC has a lot of foreign students—a lot from Jamaica, Bulgaria, and some from Africa. I like that there are so many international students."

Q "Speaking in racial terms, not very. In ethnic terms, we get many exchange students and people from different backgrounds. **Geographically, most students are from the Pennsylvania, New York, Connecticut, New Jersey area.** And ideologically, the student population is mixed, but the professors have a liberal bend to them."

Q **"Diverse and Ithaca has very little correlation**. I don't think that it's because Ithaca doesn't try to be diverse, but because Ithaca is such a small area."

Q "It's not that diverse because it's mainly white, but many of the different cultural groups have clubs, so **you can meet all different kinds of people."**

Q **"Ithaca College is devoid of any diversity,** both culturally and intellectually."

Q **"This campus is very diverse when it comes to people's interests and sexuality.** However, from a racial, religious and ideological standpoint, there is lacking diversity. It's ok, though, you roll with it and bring out what's missing in your own way. That's how Ithaca College students do it."

Q "The college insists it's very diverse, and I suppose it is compared to other schools, but minorities still tend to stand out a bit. About half the black students seem to be from Jamaica and there are a ton of Bulgarians as well. **I don't find too many Hispanics,** though there are a fair amount of Asians and Europeans."

The College Prowler Take On...
Diversity

With eighty-seven percent of IC students classifying themselves as white, the college is far from being racially diverse. Some students complain about a lack of ideological diversity, others think the college needs to attract more international students. From a U.S. geographic perspective, students come from all over the country to attend IC, leading to a good mix of views and opinions from within the states. Most students come from middle to upper-middle class households, but students' religions and sexual orientations seem to be very diverse.

Through efforts like the Martin Luther King Jr. Scholar Program, the college is trying to attract a more diverse student body. Departments such as the Office of Multicultural Affairs and the Center for the Study of Culture, Race, and Ethnicity strive to bring and showcase diversity on campus. The school sponsors different events such as Latino Heritage Month, Black History Month, and "Gaypril" to increase awareness of others on campus. IC also offers various culture courses, trying to fill the void that remains on campus. With all of the work IC is putting towards creating a more diverse campus, it should pay off sometime in the near future.

The College Prowler™ Grade on
Diversity: C

A high grade in Diversity indicates that ethnic minorities and international students have a notable presence on campus and that students of different economic backgrounds, religious beliefs, and sexual preferences are well-represented.

Guys & Girls

The Lowdown On...
Guys & Girls

Men Undergrads:
57%

Women Undergrads:
43%

Birth Control Available?
Yes, at Hammond Health Center. The Health Center offers condoms for sale, and women can get oral, patch, or injection birth control there as well.

Most Prevalent STDs on Campus
In the 2002-2003 academic year, the Health Center treated sixteen cases of Chlamydia, fifteen cases of Genital Warts/HPV, six cases of Gential Herpes, and one case of Gonorrhea.

Social Scene

Like anywhere, IC has many different varieties of people. From the extreme introvert to the life of EVERY party, any kind of person can be seen on campus. Most students are rather outgoing, and with only 6,400 students, it's hard to go anywhere without running into someone you know. On the weekends, students do anything from watch movies, shop, go ice skating, play a game of football, or hang out in a bar or club. Sometimes instead of getting dressed up, going out, and getting drunk, nothing is more fun than a movie night with some of your closest friends.

Hookups or Relationships?

There are both hookups and relationships at IC. On Monday mornings you can hear people talking about their weekend one-night stands, and then you'll see two seniors holding hands who've been together since freshmen year. It seems that there are two extremes on campus: random hookups and serious dating. There's not a lot of casual dating, but most long-term relationships happen with someone who's not an IC student. Most students who are engaged or thinking about getting engaged are dating someone from home or another school.

Best Place to Meet Guys/Girls

While some couples meet at parties, clubs, or bars, a lot meet through mutual friends, when living in the same residence hall, or while participating in something they are both interested in, like a club or an organization. Through group projects and assignments or just normal discussion in class, many phone numbers and AOL Instant Messenger screen names are exchanged. Many students have found that the relationships that last the longest are the ones that start with a common interest, rather than a random conversation at a bar.

Did You Know?

Top Places to Find Hotties:
1. The Fitness Center
2. Off-campus parties
3. Clubs

Top Places to Hookup:

1. Fifth floor of the library
2. The waterfalls
3. Near the observatory
4. Duck pond by Muller Chapel
5. Empty rooms on campus

Dress Code:

From pajama pants and sweats to skirts and khakis, anything is acceptable in class. **The earlier or later the class, the more comfortable the clothing gets.** At Ithaca, there are the typical Abercrombie & Fitch and Gap guys and girls, and then there are the people who choose to wear only black. Unless someone wears something totally outrageous, most people don't even give that student a second look. One piece of clothing that has a place in everyone's closet: an IC hooded sweatshirt.

Students Speak Out On...
Guys & Girls

"Like any college, it just depends on who you hang out with. There are many different groups, so almost anyone can find a group to hang out with."

Q "I think last year **we were voted number two by Playboy for the school with the hottest girls**. There are a lot of skinny girls here, if you think that's hot. I think it all just depends on preference, but there isn't an over-abundance of trolls roaming around campus, if that's what you what to know."

Q "Lot's of alternative people here, very few abercrombie-esque models. **It's an OK mix, with lots of girls.**"

Q "I heard once that Ithaca had the third hottest girls of any campus in the United States. **I can't say I've noticed an abnormally large number of attractive men or women**, but there are certainly a handful of attractive people in each class."

Q "**Everyone's pretty good-looking here**, I'd say a good sixty-five percent of the student body population can be considered hot."

Q "Because the homosexual statistic is so high here at IC I find that when I'm interested in a guy, besides asking whether or not he has a girlfriend, **I need to ask myself if he's gay**. It's not a bad thing, though. I have a lot of gay friends and I love them to death. Sometime they are the best people to talk to about anything because they can understand and sympathize better."

Q "**You can find hot girls at pretty much any school you go to.** There are a lot of hot girls at Ithaca College, but hopefully you aren't basing your college decision on what a bunch of college kids say about the opposite sex."

Q "Guys in Park are either funny and nice print/film guys or cute/arrogant broadcast guys. Yuck. **I've found business majors to be attractive,** but they are studying business at an unaccredited school, so that worries me."

Q "Apparently we were voted as having really good looking girls. It does surprise me sometimes that **there are so many good looking people here**. Truthfully, I hope that you aren't coming here for that, because I wouldn't want you here if that was the case."

Q "**Everyone is wonderful, period.** The personalities are what make this campus interesting and fun."

Q "If you're a gay girl or guy, this is the place to go. **Sometimes it seems like half the population is homosexual.** I've heard that Ithaca College got put on a list (possibly by Playboy) that said we had really hot girls. That's fairly true, and the guys aren't bad either, you just have to make sure you get the right sexuality. I have no trouble finding guys to drool over."

Q "I haven't seen serious promiscuity in most places. **People are fairly private,** but if you go to live shows or bands you'll see people having too much to drink and hooking up, but the bar scene tends to be fairly casual."

The College Prowler Take On...
Guys & Girls

Many students go to college expecting they'll find the love of their life, their true soul mate, the person they want to spend the rest of their life with, but many times at IC that doesn't happen. Most relationships turn into random hookups, and without a lot of casual dating, it can be hard to get to know someone. Many students bring long-term relationships to college with them and actually stay in them. With girls outnumbering guys on campus three to two, many single girls complain that the guys are either all taken or are gay. But the guys don't complain too much. Some say that Playboy once rated IC with having some of the hottest girls in the country, but hard evidence of that is hard to come by.

With a campus that's very open to sex and any sexual orientation, if someone wants to be promiscuous, he or she can find plenty of opportunities to do just that. If students want to try and find serious significant others, they can do that as well. One saying heard around campus is, "Ithaca to bed, Cornell to wed." Many feel that while that some Cornell students have more brains, the students at Ithaca have the upper hand when it comes to looks. While each guy and girl at IC doesn't take your breath away, and sometimes it's hard to get a good look at people through all the winter clothes, there are definitely those who make you want to stop and stare.

The College Prowler™ Grade on
Guys: B+

A high grade for Guys indicates that the male population on campus is attractive, smart, friendly, and engaging, and that the school has a decent ratio of guys to girls.

The College Prowler™ Grade on
Girls: A-

A high grade for Girls not only implies that the women on campus are attractive, smart, friendly, and engaging, but also that there is a fair ratio of girls to guys.

Athletics

The Lowdown On...
Athletics

Athletic Division:
NCAA Division III

Conference:
Empire 8

Eastern College Athletic
Conference

Intercollegiate Varsity Sports
Men's Teams:

Baseball
Basketball
Crew
Cross-country
Football
Indoor track
Lacrosse
Outdoor track
Soccer
Swimming
Tennis
Wrestling

Women's Teams:
Basketball
Crew
Cross-country
Field hockey
Gymnastics
Indoor track
Lacrosse
Outdoor track
Soccer
Softball
Swimming
Tennis
Volleyball

Club Sports:
Adventure Recreation
Breakdancing
Capoeira
Cheerleading
Dance
Equestrian
Fencing
Field Hockey
Hip Hop Dance Ensemble
Ice Hockey
Lacrosse
Orgullo Latino
Rugby
Seido Karate

Club Sports (*Continued...*)
Skateboarding
Skiing
Soccer
Sword
Tae Kwan Do
Ultimate Frisbee
Unbound Dance
Volleyball
Tap Dance

Intramurals:
Softball
Arena Football
Sand Volleyball
Outdoor Soccer
Tennis
6-Person Volleyball
4-Person Volleyball
Golf
Flag Football
5-Person Basketball
3-Person Basketball
Badminton
Indoor Soccer
Floor Hockey
Quickball

Fields:

Butterfield Stadium
(football, track)

Upper Terrace Lacrosse Field

Kostrinski Softball Field

Wood W. Lacrosse

Soccer Field

Freeman Baseball Fields

Yavit Field Hockey Field

Allen Fields

Ben Light Gymnasium

Hill Center Pool

Tennis Courts

Boathouse/Inlet

School Mascot:

Bombers

Getting Tickets

Students can get into any sporting event free of charge. With low attendances at many games, you're usually guaranteed a seat.

Most Popular Sport

Football

Overlooked Teams

Women's Gymnastics and Swimming

Best Place to Take a Walk

Most of the local gorges have beautiful trails that are the perfect activity for a nice day. Try Taughannock Falls and Buttermilk Falls.

Gyms/Facilities

Fitness Center
The Fitness Center, opened in 1999, is a state-of-the-art facility. The Center has something for everyone who wants to work out: free weights, cardiovascular machines, two gyms, an aerobic room and an outdoor pool.

The Hill Center
The Hill Center holds practices for various teams on campus and has an indoor pool that students can use. Indoor athletic events also take place in the Hill Center, in the Ben Light Gymnasium.

Students Speak Out On...
Athletics

"Sports aren't a huge deal. Other than Cortaca Jug, most students aren't that interested in football. Students attend games to watch their friends play, but I wouldn't say that sports are that big on campus since we are only a Division III school."

Q **"Everyone goes to Cortaca Jug** but that's about it, unless you know someone on the team."

Q "**Sports aren't too big**, except for Cortaca Jug, the annual football rivalry between Ithaca College and Cortland State University of New York. Just about everyone on campus attends that game."

Q "We are a spirited school, and **I think all sports are well participated."**

Q "**Varsity isn't a huge deal since we're only D-III**, but I've heard of a lot of students who really like intramural sports."

Q "There are many intramural sports on campus, and it's great to participate. The varsity sports are solid, but unlike big state schools, they are not the focus of the entertainment or monetary funds at Ithaca, which is good. **The football season has one big game, the Cortaca Jug,** that attracts about 12,000 people."

Q "Football is definitely big here. The Cortaca Jug game between IC and Cortland is the biggest game of the year. It's crazy. This year it was held at IC and people seriously get so plastered and wasted during pre-game and post-game that it was ridiculous. **The animosity and competition that exists between the teams is unbelievable."**

Q "With the exception of the Cortaca Jug, **nobody on campus really cares about college athletics,** except for the athletes themselves."

Q "Sports at IC can be as big or as small as you want them to be. **I don't go to many of the games,** but people who do get really into them. I also haven't joined any intramural sports, but again, people who do love it."

Q "Nobody cares, except for football season. **The football team is pretty good."**

Q "Varsity sports are not too big of a deal on campus, but athletes enjoy their fair share of fans. Intramural sports are very enjoyable, from what I hear, and **there are a broad range of sports for people to choose from."**

Q "**Sports aren't that big on campu**s, but there's always a game going on. If you're a sports fan, there are plenty of opportunities to catch a football or basketball game."

The College Prowler Take On...
Athletics

In the 2001-2002 academic year, the Bombers placed second in the country for Division III schools for the Sears Cup, which combines the results of all athletic teams from individual schools and ranks the total score against others in the schools' division. In 2002, the women's softball team won the national championship for Division III, the Bombers' football team made NCAA playoffs in 2003, and many athletes are consistently ranked nationally. Despite the talent some of the teams at IC have, students fail to attend games or show school spirit. For the students who don't want to commit to joining a varsity team, IC offers many intramural and club sports that are very popular.

It's hard to get excited about being a Bomber. The most well-attended sporting event at IC is the November football game between IC and the State University of New York at Cortland. Known as the Cortaca Jug, which Sports Illustrated has called the "Biggest little game in the nation," this rivalry game brings almost every IC student to the stadium. Other than this one Saturday afternoon, support for the teams is almost nonexistent. If someone wants to go to a school that is big on athletics, that person can appreciate all the talent that IC athletes have and try to forget about the student body's poor game attendance rating. The college administration doesn't stress athletics, and the school's overall lackluster spirit shows it. The talent and athletic opportunities are there—students just have to take part in Bomber pride.

The College Prowler™ Grade on

Athletics: C

A high grade in Athletics indicates that students have school spirit, that sports programs are respected, that games are well-attended, and that intramurals are a prominent part of student life.

Nightlife

The Lowdown On...
Nightlife

Club and Bar Prowler:
Popular Nightlife Spots!

Benchwarmers Sports Bar & Grill

214 E. State St., the Commons, Ithaca

(607) 277-7539

When Benchwarmers first opened in Ithaca, they were the only restaurant to serve burgers, and they're still known for them. They've also won numerous wing competitions for their meaty wings. Topped with a drink and watching the game on one of the many televisions, a fun time is had by all.

Benchwarmers (*Continued..*)

Specials: Monday: 20 cent wings 6 p.m.-10 p.m., 9 p.m.-close Bud Light pitchers $4.00

Tuesday: $2.00 drafts, well drinks, bottles

Wednesday: $1.50 Blue and Blue Light bottles

Thursday: $2.00 pints

Friday-Saturday: $1.00 mugs of Blue of Bud Light

Sunday: Noon-4 p.m. $3.00 Bloody Mary, noon-close four bottles of Blue or Bud Light in ice bucket for $7.00

→

Castaways

413 Taughannock Blvd., Ithaca

(607) 272-1370

http://www.castawaysithaca.
com

Castaways is located along
the waterfront and is a popular
place to kick back and have
some fun. Before the music
starts, enjoy good food at
good prices on the club's
outside deck. Castaways
features live music Thursday
through Saturday and themed
music nights Sunday through
Wednesday.

Specials: Sunday-Saturday: 4
p.m.-7 p.m. happy hour

Common Ground

1230 Danby Road, Ithaca

(607) 273-1505

http://www.
ithacacommonground.com

Common Ground is a
progressive dance club,
open to men and women of
all ages, nationalities, and
sexual orientations, featuring
latin, swing, tango, and Top
40 music. While it can be
classified as a gay club, many
straight students go there just
to have a good time.

Specials: Although Common
Ground has weekly specials,
it's advised to check out their
website for other events.

Wednesday: Chicken Wing
Special, 5 p.m.-8 p.m. Buffalo
style chicken wings are only
fifteen cents each.

Thursday: Coors Light Night.
Only $1.50 all night long.

Dunbar's

409 Eddy St., Ithaca

(607) 216-0904

Dunbar's is known by many as
the place to go after a Cornell
hockey game, and after a
victory, it can get pretty rowdy.

Specials: Wednesday: "Group
Therapy" six shots and a
pitcher of beer for $5.00.

The Haunt

702 Willow Ave., Ithaca

(607) 275-3447

http://www.thehaunt.com

Every Saturday night, The
Haunt attracts nearly 500
people to their eighties dance
party. The club features live
music at least three nights a
week.

Specials: Tuesday-Thursday: 4
p.m.-7 p.m. happy hour

Friday: 4 p.m.-8 p.m. happy
hour

Micawber's

118 N. Aurora St., Ithaca

(607) 273-9243

Micawber's is an Irish pub that
is popular with regulars and
people downtown during the
day, but at night it turns into
a very lively place filled with
college students. Most specials
vary from week to week, but
Micawber's is known for their
themed parties, such as the
ones for Mardi Gras and St.
Patrick's Day.

Specials: Monday-Friday: 15
minute special, 5:15 p.m.-5:30
p.m., half-off drinks

Moonshadow Tavern

114 The Commons, Ithaca

(607) 273-8741

This is a popular place for IC students to go to have a good time, and their specials are great for those on a budget.

Specials: Wednesday: 10 p.m.-1 a.m. 3 for 1 deal on all mug and well drinks.

Saturday: 10 p.m.-1 a.m. 3 for 1 deal for use on your next visit

The Nines

311 College Ave., Ithaca

(607) 272-1888

http://www.theninesithacany.com

The Nines has some of the greatest pizza around, and it's great place to relax, listen to some music, and do a little dancing. With some talented bands taking the stage, The Nines attracts many college students who want to leave the hectic world of college life behind.

Speicals: Sunday-Saturday: 4 p.m.-7 p.m. happy hour

Rulloff's

411 College Ave., Ithaca

(607) 272-6067

Playboy named Rulloff's the February 2004 college bar of the month. While the clientele is mostly Cornell students, this Collegetown establishment draws a variety of people.

Specials: Sunday: Happy hour all day

Monday: Karaoke Night with Michelob Light and Michelob Ultra $1.50

Tuesday: Rail Drinks, Heineken, and Amstel Light $2.00

Wednesday: $6.00 Labatt's pitchers, $1.50 Labatt's bottles

Student Favorites:

Monshadow Tavern

The Haunt

Micawber's

The Nines

Castaways

Useful Resources for Nightlife:

http://www.ithacatimes.com

http://www.theithacajournal.com

http://www.ithacaevents.com

Bars Close At:
1 a.m.

Primary Areas with Nightlife:
Collegetown
The Commons

Cheapest Place to Get a Drink:
Moonshadow Tavern

Local Specialties:
Ithaca Pale Ale
Ithaca Beer

Favorite Drinking Games:
Beer Pong
Card Games
Flip Cup
Sh*t

Other Places to Check Out:
Chapter House
Chanticleer
O'Leary's Irish Pub
Kelly's Dock-Side Café
Republica

Club Crawler

Most clubs around Ithaca are filled with IC and Cornell students, looking to have a good time after a busy week. Students have to be at least eighteen to get in, and some nights the clubs will only permit students over twenty-one. Make sure to call ahead to find out the event and the minimum age requirement.

Bar Prowler

There are a number of bars in the Ithaca area, and the following are quite popular with IC students. Students take advantage of the great drink and food specials that the bars have to offer.

What to Do if You're Not 21

Besides the dance clubs that the twenty-one-and-under crowd is permitted in, Ithaca has a number of bowling alleys, movie theaters, shopping areas, and different cafes and restaurants that are popular with all ages.

Students Speak Out On...
Nightlife

"Most students who party go to the frat parties at Cornell, or at off-campus houses. Some students have parties in their apartments, but not as many. Kelly's and Castaways are the clubs off campus that many students attend."

Q "**Parties will inevitably be over by 11:30**, so go out early and be prepared to walk, or run, as the case may be."

Q "**Parties on campus are lame**, but I don't really like parties anyway."

Q "The nightlife in Ithaca pretty much consists of the bar scene. **The clubbing scene came and went** with Semesters being shut down last year, and since then no other club has really come in to try the market yet."

Q "For a good time, head to a Cornell frat party. A lot of people live on Pennsylvania Ave. and Coddington (Road), and I've heard they throw huge parties. Like I said, I don't party, but I've heard good things about Kelly's and Castaways. **For more of a low-key night, the Nines in Collegetown is a great place to relax** and listen to local bands."

Q "**Clubs:** The Haunt and Kelly's; Parties: Coddington, Hillview, Kendall, or Pennsylvania."

Q "As a freshman, I spent most of my time going to parties in the Cornell fraternity district. There are parties in the Ithaca Collegetown (a.k.a. the IC Ghetto), but rest assured, **these parties will be broken up by midnight.** By sophomore year, most people tend to go to gatherings thrown by friends at their apartments, because the en-masse party scene eventually gets really old."

Q "Parties on campus are great, despite the fact that you can't fit too many people in a room and you can't be too loud, but that's part of what makes the whole evening intimate. **The bars and clubs off campus are very lively** with loud music and plentiful supplies of alcohol."

Q "**It's hit or miss for parties on campus.** I can only recommend Micawber's as a good bar."

Q "There seems to be a party every weekend on this campus. Some of the streets out the back entrance of campus are totally populated by students, so **house parties are common.**"

Q "There is no shortage of things to do in Ithaca at night or on the weekends (It's great to be in a college town.) There are lots of bars and cafés, both on the Commons and in Collegetown. There are also a few dance clubs, although there are fewer now than when I first came to college. **Eighties night at the Haunt on Saturdays is always popular.** There are always several places where you can go to see live music, usually local bands."

Q "One of the only problems I see with the nightlife is that **there aren't really any bars within walking distance of the college**. You could walk to the Commons if you wanted to, but walking back up the hill is heck. There are buses that run from the college to downtown, but they stop operating fairly early, so you either need a designated driver or cab fare. A lot of places are over twenty-one, but some are eighteen and over if you don't want to drink."

The College Prowler Take On...
Nightlife

If Cornell and IC students have one thing in common, it's that they both know how to have a good time. Living in a college town has definite perks. Bars and taverns line the streets, and students find parties to attend very easily. Since walking back up the hill can be hard when someone has had too much to drink, most IC students don't walk to bars. That means they either have to take the bus or have a designated driver. The clubs have a variety of themed music nights and attract talented local bands for live music. While there are some parties on campus in apartments or cramped dorm rooms, students tend to go off campus to find a place to party. House parties are an every weekend occurrence, and frat parties at Cornell are popular with the under twenty-one crowd at IC. In their first few weeks on campus, many freshmen are eager to experience "college life" and head to Cornell to get drunk. The beer is cheap, and the opposite sex is eager, but many IC students outgrow the phase and find other places to go.

While on some nights the under twenty-one crowd isn't permitted in clubs, college freshmen and sophomores can find an abundance of things to do and places to go. Many students carry fake IDs to drink at bars or get into shows, but it's not recommended. For those of legal age, bars like Micawber's and Benchwarmers know what students want and offer plenty of specials to keep the students coming back happy. If you're looking for a good time, you're guaranteed to find it at IC.

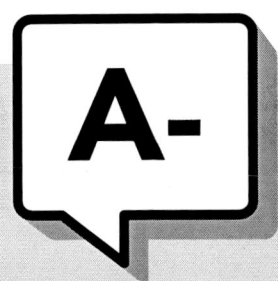

The College Prowler™ Grade on
Nightlife: A-

A high grade in Nightlife indicates that there are many bars and clubs in the area that are easily accessible and affordable. Other determining factors include the number of options for the under-21 crowd and the prevalence of house parties.

Greek Life

The Lowdown On...
Greek Life

Number of Fraternities:
4

Number of Sororities:
0

Percent of Undergrad Men in Fraternities:
1

Percent of Undergrad Women in Sororities:
1

Fraternities on Campus:
Mu Phi Epsilon
Kappa Gamma Psi
Phi Mu Alpha Sinfonia
Sigma Alpha Iota

Other Greek Organizations:
Interfraternity Council

Students Speak Out On...
Greek Life

"As far as I know there is only some music fraternity and maybe one other small one. We don't really have Greek life. If you want to get involved in that, you can walk over to Cornell."

Q "**No Greek life.** I like it that way."

Q "There are a few underground sororities and fraternities, but **most people think they're stupid.**"

Q "**There are no official fraternities or sororities other than academic ones.** They absolutely do not dominate the social scene."

Q "There isn't really Greek life on the campus. **The college does not promote it,** and there are few sororities or fraternities for the college."

Q "The only fraternities associated with the college are professional and musical fraternities. Unlike most colleges, **fraternities do not dominate the social scene** at Ithaca College."

Q "There is no Greek life. **There are underground fraternities and sororities,** but they do not do that much. As far as I know, Greek life is nothing here."

Q "The college doesn't endorse any official fraternities or sororities, but **there are a few unofficial ones**. You don't really pay much attention to them in general and it doesn't seem that most people care about them."

Q **"Greek like here is nearly dead**, which isn't necessarily a bad thing."

The College Prowler Take On...
Greek Life

Forget about joining Delta Kappa Epsilon, Alpha Sigma Phi or Alpha Kappa Alpha while attending Ithaca College. After a student died in a fraternity-related drinking incident in 1980, the college banned all fraternities and sororities. While some "underground" Greek life occurs on campus, the college refuses to recognize any of the social groups. If students yearn to participate in Greek festivities, they can visit Cornell University, which is just on the other side of town, to socialize with Cornell's sixty fraternities and sororities.

Many students don't realize the lack of Greek life on campus until they arrive for their freshmen year. It may be disappointing for some, but many students appreciate the fact that there are no social fraternities at IC. The few professional fraternities on campus have no real presence; most students don't even know of them.

The College Prowler™ Grade on

Greek Life: D

A high grade in Greek Life indicates that sororities and fraternities are not only present, but also active on campus. Other determining factors include the variety of houses available and the respect the Greek community receives from the rest of the campus.

Drug Scene

The Lowdown On...
Drug Scene

Most Prevalent Drugs on Campus:

Alcohol

Marijuana

In 2002:
Liquor-Related Referrals:

448

Liquor-Related Arrests:

18

Drug-Related Referrals:

158

Drug-Related Arrests:

18

Drug Counseling Programs:

The Counseling Center

Ground Floor, Hammond Health Center

(607) 274-3136

Students Speak Out On...
Drug Scene

"It's a hippie school, what do you think? Follow your nose and the slight wisp of smoke. Lots of pot, that's all I've really come in contact with."

Q "Pot is around a lot. I haven't had much experience with people doing much else. **I wouldn't say that harder drugs are used a lot on campus.**"

Q "**Marijuana is very prevalent,** but I haven't seen or heard of too many people engaging in harder drugs."

Q "Ithaca is very liberal. I don't know if anyone uses any hard-core drugs, but I do know that marijuana is prevalent here. **I've also heard of people abusing prescription drugs like Adderall.**"

Q "**I think that drugs are prevalent on almost any campus**. I think that the biggest drug-related problem that we have to deal with is marijuana."

Q "**Marijuana is the hardest drug** most people at Ithaca College use, and for most, marijuana use is a phase."

Q "People smoke marijuana frequently, and I am not aware of other widespread drug use. **I had a pot head for a roommate freshman year.**"

Q "You know what, I'm oblivious to the drug scene. Apparently there was a big scene at my high school that people from other schools informed me about after I graduated, but I didn't see it. **If you're into that, it's college.** I am sure there is something out there. If you aren't into that, there are plenty of people who are just as oblivious as myself."

Q "Yes, there are a lot of drugs here. Pot is the most heavily used drug, then shrooms, then opium. **There are some harder drugs, but they're seldom used**. If you do not want to do drugs and you want to stay away from all illegal activity, it is very easy to do so here."

Q "**Drugs are everywhere**—like you wouldn't believe. Half of my floor smokes pot and for a while the campus police were coming three or four times a week. From what I hear, pot and hallucinogens are very easy to get in town."

Q "I don't know about any hard core drugs, but **marijuana is fairly common**, especially given the pot signs in the downtown Commons shops. They sell some very pretty bongs, bowls, hookahs, etc. You get the idea."

Q "**The prevalence of drugs on campus is rather discerning**. I know many, many people who use drugs and it is disturbing and upsetting."

The College Prowler Take On...
Drug Scene

There's no doubt about it that IC students partake in the use of illegal substances. There are even times where students go to class high, or smoke pot in public places. The Princeton Review even "honored" IC, ranking the college 14th in the "Reefer Madness" category. This is not to say that all students at IC are pot heads, or even close to it. If students don't want to have any run-ins with drugs during their four years at IC, it is totally possible to do so. If students want to find someplace to get high every night of the week, that can happen as well. IC is not a dry campus, meaning that students are permitted to have alcohol on campus if they are over twenty-one. The under-twenty-one crowd does its fair share of drinking as well, but once again, if someone wants to, he or she doesn't have to touch a drop of alcohol while at IC. Mainly, it's up to the individuals to decide what kind of lifestyles they want to lead.

Although a number of students use illegal substances or drink before they turn twenty-one, the scene isn't so prevalent to make other students uncomfortable if they want to be drug-free. IC is a school where if you don't want to associate with the drug scene, it's fine. The Health Center's drug counseling program is there to help students if they need it, and public safety officers work to control any substance problem that arises on campus.

The College Prowler™ Grade on

Drug Scene: C-

A high grade in the Drug Scene indicates that drugs are not a noticeable part of campus life; drug use is not visible, and no pressure to use them seems to exist.

Campus Strictness

The Lowdown On...
Campus Strictness

What Are You Most Likely to Get Caught Doing on Campus?
- Underage drinking
- Smoking marijuana
- Downloading and sharing music files
- Parking illegally
- Creating a disturbance

Students Speak Out On...
Campus Strictness

"In comparison to most colleges our size, our school is very lenient on drugs and drinking. It takes three or four offenses in a year before the school decides to really discipline you, and most of the time you will get off with little more than a warning."

Q "The town cops pretty much just tell you to go home, unless you are being ridiculous. **The campus police will bust you** for underage drinking and drugs, though."

Q "**Resident Assistants are required to write up incidents of underage drinking**, and students caught drinking generally get judicially referred."

Q "The use of drugs is clearly punished more severely than underage drinking. The police generally intervene only when someone reports the odor of marijuana or a rowdy party. **RAs are responsible for upholding IC alcohol policies on a regular basis** and police only get involved under more severe conditions, like a huge party in a dorm room that the RA can't control on his own."

Q "If you want to party, **I'd recommend going off campus to avoid public safety** and getting written up."

Q "**If you get caught, you'll be in trouble.** I don't think they go to great extents to catch you, but like I said, they take it seriously if they see it."

Q "IC takes drugs very seriously. **If you are caught with illegal substances there are penalties."**

Q "**It's thankfully not a dry campus**, so as long as they don't actually see you with a drink they won't do anything to you. As long as you're not loud or causing trouble, they don't care if you're drinking."

Q "On a Saturday night around 2 a.m. my friend and I had to wake up our RA because some people were smoking pot in their room and it lingered throughout the hall and bathroom. **The RA called campus safety and they played it off as if nothing was going on.** It was upsetting."

The College Prowler Take On...
Campus Strictness

Drug and alcohol policies are pretty strict on campus, but the officers are always willing to work with people and to help them out, rather than simply punishing the students for their behavior. There is a lot of underage drinking that happens on campus, but because it's not a dry campus, it can be hard to crack down on what really is illegal. The campus is extremely strict when it comes to parking; park in the wrong lot and you're guaranteed a twenty dollar ticket. If the officers really catch you doing something wrong, you'll get written up for it, but the penalties aren't that severe. All write-ups get handled by Judicial Affairs. The Resident Assistants have huge jobs. Not only do they provide help for the students on their floor, but the RAs have to go on rounds to make sure the entire building is safe.

The students who complain that public safety is too strict are the ones who are getting busted. The students who complain that public safety needs to crack down even more are the ones who abide by all the rules. If students see something that's not supposed to be happening, they should call public safety, and something will be done about it. Many students fail to remember that the officers are here to protect the students, not to bust them.

The College Prowler™ Grade on

Campus Strictness: B

A high Campus Strictness grade implies an overall lenient atmosphere; police and RAs are fairly tolerant, and the administration's rules are flexible.

Parking

The Lowdown On...
Parking

Student Parking Lot?
Yes

Freshman Allowed to Park?
Yes

Parking Permit Cost:
$100 for upperclassmen
$200 for freshmen

IC Parking Services:
(607) 274-3333
http://www.ithaca.edu/safety/tbmain.htm

Common Parking Tickets:
Permit Violation: $20
No Parking Zone: $30
Handicapped Zone: $100
Fire Lane: $40

Parking Permits

Within the first week of classes, or whenever you bring your vehicle to campus, go to the public safety building located on the north end of campus and fill out the necessary paperwork. For the first few days of classes, be prepared for a long line.

Best Places to Find a Parking Spot

The old freshmen lot next to Emerson Hall and the lot across Route 96B usually have a place to park at any time of the day.

Good Luck Getting a Parking Spot Here

In front of the Communications School in the afternoon

Students Speak Out On...
Parking

> "Parking isn't too bad; it depends on when you go, though. Right before Tuesday and Thursday afternoon classes the parking lots are insane."

Q "Find a spot and **stay there.**"

Q "It depends on the time. In the middle of the day there is never anywhere to park in the student lots, at least not ones close to where you want to be. Once it gets later, more spots open up, but **it does take a few trips around the lot** most of the time to find a spot."

Q "Now that they raised the price of upperclassmen to park, **there are a lot more spots open**. I never leave campus during the day because when there are classes going on, it's impossible to find a spot."

Q "**Parking is very difficult**, especially during class times."

Q "The parking scene is a little crowded, but at least in the Gardens it is manageable. **You might have to park a fair distance from home,** but at least you have a space."

Q "The parking here is way too small. IC underestimates the amount of people that bring cars. Also, **the parking space available for each class is ridiculous.** It's insane that freshmen have to park in the Emerson lots, especially if most of them live in the upper quads."

Q "Parking is not easy to find, and it's expensive. You need to pay to have your car on campus, and **it's not cheap."**

Q **"Parking can be a hassle**. Winter just worsens it with all the snow making it difficult to pull into and out of spots, and sometimes reducing the number of parking places. Often you'll end up parking in a gravel parking lot."

Q "It is very convenient having a car on campus, but Parking Services are very difficult to deal with and the rules and regulations are ridiculous. Aside from that, there are few parking spots on campus, and both lots designated for freshman only are on the outskirts of campus. Also, **$200 is a lot of money for a parking permit** and if you add that to the $20 each you have to pay every time you get a parking ticket, it gets expensive."

The College Prowler Take On...
Parking

It's sometimes nearly impossible to find a parking place from 9 a.m.-3 p.m. on campus, and when one is found, it's usually a bit of a walk to class. When the snow is plowed, the piles of it take away even more of the available parking spots. In an effort to keep freshmen from bringing cars to campus, the first-year students must pay $200 for a parking permit, double what the upperclassmen pay. IC students are somewhat lucky, because many schools won't allow freshmen to have cars on campus at all, but all freshmen are required to park in designated lots. The freshmen lots are very inconvenient for those first-year students who live in the Towers or Terraces, because the lots are on the other side of campus. If you park in a lot you're not supposed to, you're almost guaranteed to have a ticket awaiting you underneath your windshield wiper when you get back to your car.

After 3 p.m. on weekdays it's easy to find parking spaces, but that doesn't help the students who live off campus and start their day at 1 p.m. The parking situation could be worse, but it's manageable. When you have to be someplace at a certain time, just make sure to allot time to find a place to park.

The College Prowler™ Grade on

Parking: C+

A high grade in this section indicates that parking is both available and affordable, and that parking enforcement isn't overly severe.

Transportation

The Lowdown On...
Transportation

Ways to Get Around Town

Public Transportation

Tompkins Consolidated Area Transit (TCAT), (607) 277-7433; Pick up schedules from the Information Desk in the Campus Center or visit http://www.tcatbus.com.

Taxi Cabs

Blue Light Cab Company, (607) 277-2227

Cayuga Taxi, (607) 277-8294

Ithaca Dispatch, Inc., (607) 277-8294

University Taxi, (607) 277-7777

Car Rentals

Avis, local: (607) 257-0441; national: (800) 831-2847, http://www.avis.com

Enterprise, local: (607) 275-9000; national: (800) 736-8222, http://www.enterprise.com

Hertz, local: (607) 275-0019; national: (800) 654-3131, http://www.hertz.com

National, local: (607) 272-2575; national: (800) 227-7368, http://www.nationalcar.com

→

Best Ways to Get Around Town:

Drive, or find a friend who does

TCAT

A bike

Ways to Get Out of Town:

Airlines Serving Ithaca:

US Airways, (800) 428-4322, http://www.usairways.com

Airlines Serving Elmira:

US Airways, (800) 428-4322, http://www.usairways.com

Northwest, (800) 225-2525, http://www.nwa.com

Airlines Serving Binghamton:

Delta, (800) 221-1212, http://www.delta-air.com

US Airways, (800) 428-4322, http://www.usairways.com

Northwest, (800) 225-2525, http://www.nwa.com

United, (800) 241-6522, http://www.united.com

Airlines Serving Syracuse:

American Eagle, (800) 433-7300, http://www.AA.com

Comair, (800) 221-1212, http://www.comair.com

CommutAir, (800) 525-0280, http://www.commutair.com

Continental Express (800) 525-0280, http://www.continental.com

Airlines (*Continued...*)

Delta, (800) 221-1212, http://www.delta-air.com

JetBlue Airways, (800) 538-2583, http://www.jetblue.com

Northwest, (800) 225-2525, http:// http://www.nwa.com

TransMeridian Airlines, (866) 435-9862, www.transmeridian-airlines.com

United Express, (800) 241-6522, http://www.united.com

US Airways, (800) 428-4322, http://www.usairways.com

Airport:

Ithaca-Tompkins Regional Airport, (607) 257-0456

The Ithaca-Tompkins Regional Airport is located approximately ten minutes from campus.

Elmira-Corning Regional Airport (607) 795-0402

The Elmira-Corning Regional Airport is located approximately forty-five minutes from campus.

Greater Binghamton Airport, (607) 763-4471

The Greater Binghamton Regional Airport is located approximately one hour from campus.

Syracuse Hancock International Airport, (315) 454-3263

The Syracuse Hancock International Airport is located approximately one hour and fifteen minutes from campus.

How to Get There:

Airline Limousine (607) 273-3030 or (800) 273-9197. The vans or buses pick students up on campus. From IC to the Ithaca airport, it costs $12, from IC to Syracuse, it will cost $50.

Other airports have similar services. Call the airports for details.

A Cab Ride to the Ithaca Airport costs:

$10-$15

Greyhound

The Greyhound Bus Lines is located in downtown Ithaca, approximately two miles from campus. For scheduling information, call (607) 272-7930.

www.greyhound.com

Greyhound Bus Lines

710 W. State St.

Ithaca, NY 14850

Travel Agents

AAA Travel Agency, 725 S. Meadow St., Ithaca, (607) 273-6727

AIM Travel & Tours Inc., 2359 N. Triphammer Road, Ithaca, (607) 257-7223

Baker Travel, 309 N. Aurora St., Ithaca. (607) 272-2537

Council Travel, 206 B Dryden Road, Ithaca, (607) 277-0373

Liberty Travel, Pyramid Mall, Ithaca, (607) 257-0140

O'Rourke Beam Travel, 134 E. Seneca St., Ithaca, (607) 277-3133

Stone Travel Agency, 401 College Ave., Ithaca, (607) 273-4443

Stone Travel Agency, 903 Hanshaw Road, Ithaca, (607) 257-2515

Uniglobe Master Travel, 202 The Commons, Suite 406, Ithaca, (607) 277-6954, 1-800-836-8465

Students Speak Out On...
Transportation

"I've spent almost an hour numerous times waiting in the cold for the bus. If you need to get somewhere, and you don't have a car and don't know someone who does, it's the only way to get most places."

Q **"There are bus stops on campus,** but as for getting places, sometimes it takes a while."

Q "Public transportation is not convenient at all! **You generally need to leave one to two hours travel time each way to get to the mall,** which is about a five minute drive from the campus."

Q "Public transportation isn't bad. They raised the fare for the TCAT (the local bus) from $1 to $1.50 this year, but it's generally good if you just want to go to the Commons or Collegetown. It takes forever to get to the mall. **I recommend getting a ride** or borrowing a car from a friend."

Q "If you want to go right down the hill to the Commons or over to Cornell on weekdays, the bus is convenient. The schedule gets to be sporadic on weekends. **Going to the grocery store is about a one-and-a-half hour ordeal.** I'm from Florida, and because of an off-campus job and the hassle of trying to get around by bus and by rides from others, I drove up my car from home."

Q "The bus system here is very confusing and takes twice as long to get anywhere that you need to go. **The taxis here are very expensive.**"

Q "**The bus service isn't that bad** if all you want to do is go downtown, but for going to the mall or food shopping, it's inconvenient."

Q "**The bus into town runs every thirty minutes during the day, and every hour at night**. To get to and from the mall or the grocery store, however, it takes at least three hours, due to transfers and such."

Q "I have taken the bus once in one-and-a-half years, and **it was only one way.** Does that tell you something?"

Q "I got really annoyed with it last year. **It exists, and it's an experience,** but I found myself really confused and waiting a long time sometimes. I guess if you can figure it out, then it works, but you have to do your homework."

Q "**It's a pain in the butt sometimes.** To get to the mall by bus it can take up to an hour, though the mall is like fifteen minutes away. And this year they've reduced the busing schedule so it's probably worse. Taxis aren't too bad."

The College Prowler Take On...
Transportation

To discourage students from bringing their cars to campus, IC officials tell students they can get everywhere they need to go on the Tompkins Consolidated Area Transit (TCAT) buses. That part is true—if say, someone has hours to devote to getting someplace that would normally take twenty minutes roundtrip. Buses service the college, but for the most part, only stop at one place on the Commons. Then, if the rider needs to get to another place, after receiving a transfer ticket, he or she has to wait for the next bus to come. The process can take hours and usually inconveniences anyone who chooses to ride the bus. But, if you just plan on visiting the Commons, taking the TCAT works just fine.

The college offers discounted bus passes to students at $240 per academic year, but it's usually not worth it unless you plan on taking the bus often. If you need to get someplace, find a friend with a car and avoid taking the bus. Although rush hour or weekend traffic downtown and on Route 13 can get horrendous, traveling in an automobile will save you time and an even bigger headache. If students want to fly home or take the bus, the Ithaca and surrounding areas have enough options to get them anywhere, but since most of the airports are smaller, ticket prices are generally more expensive than they would be at a larger airport.

B-

The College Prowler™ Grade on

Transportation: B-

A high grade for Transportation indicates that campus buses, public buses, cabs, and rental cars are readily-available and affordable. Other determining factors include proximity to an airport and the necessity of transportation.

Weather

The Lowdown On...
Weather

Average Temperature
Fall: 49 °F
Winter: 25 °F
Spring: 44 °F
Summer: 67 °F

Average Precipitation
Fall: 3.39 in.
Winter: 2.22 in.
Spring: 3.02 in.
Summer: 3.60 in.

Students Speak Out On...
Weather

{ **"It's cold! Bring as many warm jackets as possible, along with scarves, hats, mittens, gloves, and even long underwear. Be prepared for -20 degree weather."**

Q "It is cold and windy, but also pretty during warm weather. **Layers, layers, layers!"**

Q "Lots of layers, and gloves and scarves. **The fall is really nice,** but be prepared for snow pants and boots."

Q **"Hotter than heck when you first get here in August, then it's snot freezing**, frostbite in a few minutes, and mind-numbingly cold for the rest of the year. It's only cold when the wind is blowing, though, which is pretty much all the time. Bring a few pairs of shorts for the few times it's warm, and t-shirts (for layering), sweaters, sweatshirts, long pants, winter jacket, boots, scarf, gloves, and ear-muffs, or something of the like to cover your ears, for the rest of the year."

Q "It's unbelievably cold, as in **we're excited when we reach double digits.** If you don't own a thick winter jacket, good gloves, a hat and scarf, buy them now if you plan on going to IC. There is a lot of snow, from November to April. It's also gray a lot, and windy, but you get used to it. You don't necessarily grow to like it, but you become accustomed to putting on five layers before you walk to class.

Q **"Ithaca is cold!** From November through March, there is usually a foot or more of snow on the ground. Temperatures reach -15 degrees with the wind chill. Bring warm sweaters, long underwear, and thick socks. In the summers and early fall, on the other hand, it's often very humid."

Q **"Cold, cold, cold, cold, cold, and snowy.** Bring warm layers, thick socks, and waterproof shoes!"

Q "Imagine the coldest day you have ever been in during a winter in the Northeast, lower the temperature by ten degrees, and that's what the Ithaca winter is like at its best. It is cold, snowy, and windy on South Hill. **Sweaters, jeans, cords, fleece, parkas, and boots are all encouraged.** At the beginning of the fall semester, there is still summer left, which is really nice up here. It'll be warm, even in the eighties, and most dorms do not have air conditioning, so you'll need some cool clothing. The spring, if we get one, can be similarly pleasant, although winter and its thaw has lasted here until the first week in May before."

Q **"It's very warm in late summer and early fall,** but it cools down quickly and is very cold in winter. It snows a lot during the winter, so a heavy coat, scarf, hat, gloves, and snow shoes are a must for walking to class."

Q "If it hasn't snowed by November, consider yourself lucky. For much of the 'spring' semester, you will be freezing, and **your pants will be covered in snow salt**. A hat and gloves are highly recommended."

Q **"Cold, windy, rainy, and occasionally, amazingly beautiful**. Bring it all—especially a scarf, gloves, boots, and pants you don't mind getting salty."

Q "Welcome to the winter. It's beautiful, but it can definitely get cold. **I have gotten used to it, and so long as it's not windy, I don't feel it**. I like to wear layers because they keep the building well heated, so I need to be able to strip down upon entrance."

Q "The weather changes every five minutes. It is perfect fall weather—cool and crisp. **Winters are brutal, with cold winds, ice, and snow, but it can be a lot of fun**. Spring weather arrives in mid-April. Bring all types of clothes because, like I said, you never know what temperature it will be in Ithaca."

Q **"If you attend Ithaca, you should learn to like cold weather.** I would recommend a good pair of boots and a warm coat from Lands End or Columbia. Long underwear wouldn't hurt either, if you plan to go sledding or ice skating. Bring t-shirts also, as the dorms tend to get very warm."

Q "In the beginning of the year it's not too bad, but you'll need a fan during the August and September heat because the dorms aren't air-conditioned. Once it starts snowing it pretty much doesn't stop until the end of the year. The snow takes forever to melt because it pretty much stays cold from November or December until April or May. Basically, a lot of warm clothing. **The wind is what makes it so cold most of the time,** and rain is far from uncommon. Don't expect too much sun."

The College Prowler Take On...
Weather

When students first arrive on campus in August, they find eighty degree weather and blue skies. With beautiful flowers and manicured lawns, students complete their homework sitting comfortably on the green grass. The fountains, the college's signature landmark, produce a light mist that refreshes students as they walk by, often cooling them down from the hot temperatures. In only weeks, however, Ithaca's beautiful landscape becomes anything but inviting. Snow flurries are often seen before fall break, and students should bring their winter coats to school with them in August. After fall break, the fountains are turned off, the flowers are uprooted, and the plows are ready in case of significant snowfall. In the middle of winter, students walk to early morning and evening classes in wind chills that can reach 20 or 30 degrees below zero. A good winter coat, a hat, gloves, a scarf, and waterproof shoes with traction are all needed to brave the campus.

During spring break, students bring back their sandals and shorts. In April, as the daffodils and tulips bloom, students once again venture from their dorm rooms into the outside world. It's back to sitting on the grass, taking in the campus views and eating lunch outside. The weather is so nice that it makes students want to forget about the time they spent in the "Arctic" and convince them that just maybe Ithaca isn't as bad of a place they thought it was in January.

The College Prowler™ Grade on
Weather: C

A high Weather grade designates that temperatures are mild and rarely reach extremes, that the campus tends to be sunny rather than rainy, and that weather is fairly consistent rather than unpredictable.

Report Card Summary

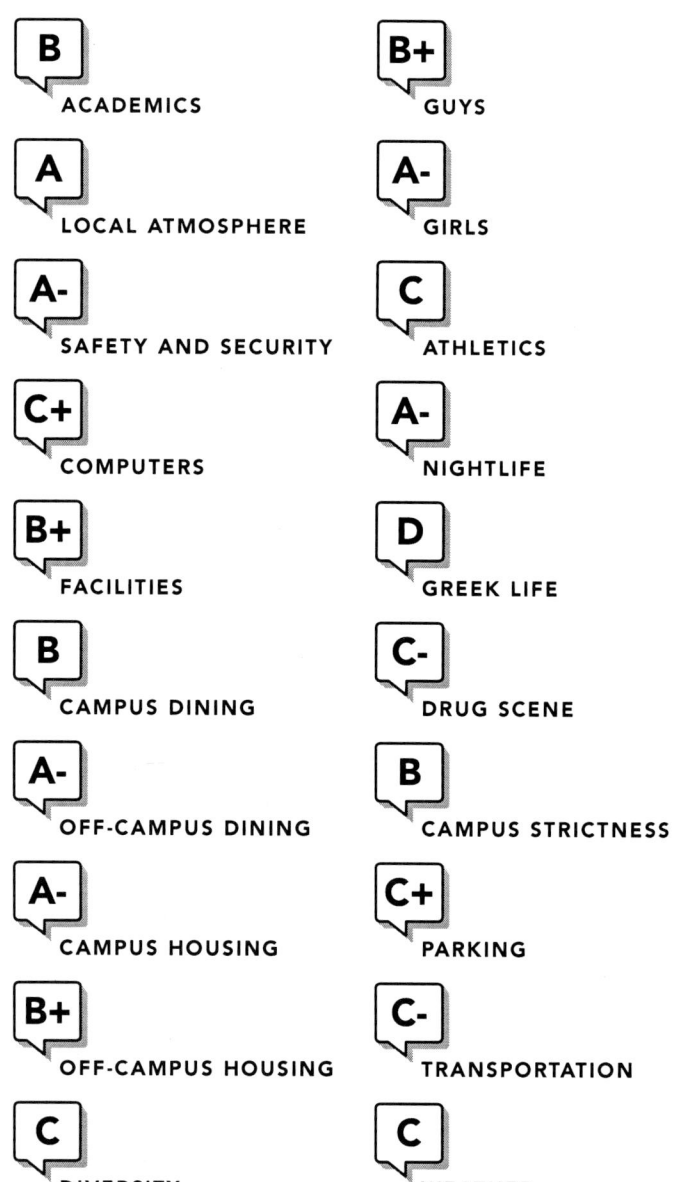

B ACADEMICS

A LOCAL ATMOSPHERE

A- SAFETY AND SECURITY

C+ COMPUTERS

B+ FACILITIES

B CAMPUS DINING

A- OFF-CAMPUS DINING

A- CAMPUS HOUSING

B+ OFF-CAMPUS HOUSING

C DIVERSITY

B+ GUYS

A- GIRLS

C ATHLETICS

A- NIGHTLIFE

D GREEK LIFE

C- DRUG SCENE

B CAMPUS STRICTNESS

C+ PARKING

C- TRANSPORTATION

C WEATHER

Overall Experience

Students Speak Out On...
Overall Experience

"I love it here. There are good opportunities to be found, with a fairly good mix of decent people. You just have to go out and find it, but that's what college is all about."

Q "I love it. I can't imagine being anywhere else. **I think this school feels like home.**"

Q "**I love it here.** The only problem I have is with the distance from my house. Ideally I'd take Ithaca and move it a few hours closer to home, but obviously I can't do that. I'm happy enough here to suffer the long car ride home."

Q "I love it here. **My overall experience has been great.** Yeah, there are things that have pissed me off with the administration and the weather and stuff, but not enough to make me want to be anywhere else."

Q "I have had good and bad experiences at Ithaca. **The weather is depressing** and the political climate is not friendly to conservatives, so there have definitely been times when I missed my home. I think I've learned a lot in my three years here, however, and I will take with me knowledge and friends that will last for the rest of my life."

Q "I've had a great experience here. **I had considered transferring,** but I held on another semester and it turns out to have been a great move. College is what you make of it. I don't think it matters where you go, as long as you're learning, meeting people, and having a good time. I've succeeded in all three at IC."

Q "As a senior, I have been reflecting on my four years here. After being an editor for the school paper, studying abroad to Russia and Washington, D.C., and surviving four especially chilly winters, I can say that **I chose the right school for me**. In high school, I was unsure of what to do for a major up until freshman orientation, when I selected journalism. Even though I have enjoyed the journalism program, I'm still not sure what I want to do as a career. It has not been a waste of time, though. The lasting friendships I have made, the connections with professors, and the experiences of living in a small town have all contributed much to my education."

Q "I'm overall very ambivalent about this school. There are definitely days where I wish I would've attended a school closer to home, but then there are days where I'm glad that I'm here. The main factor that's keeping me here is the Park School program. **It's very unique and stimulates a real-life environment.** If I could find a program like this in California (that's not theory based and then hands on), I would definitely transfer. However, I think that being so far from home has its benefits too."

Q "I liked Ithaca a lot. The campus isn't too hard to get around, and I liked the environment. However, without financial aid, **it is an expensive school to pay for out of pocket** in addition to all the costs such as books, cable, and recreation money."

Q "Although I often wonder why I didn't decide to go to school in a warmer place, I am glad that I chose my college based on what I can get out of it rather than on how nice of a place it is. **Upstate New York is a harsh place for most of the year**, but Ithaca College has so much to offer and keeps you so busy that you tend to forget about the negative aspects of the place."

Q "I had my doubts at the very beginning of freshman year, but once I found my groove I have been obsessed with school. **I even had a countdown till return over the summer.**"

Q "I absolutely love this school and cannot imagine myself any place else. It has been the most amazing opportunity to be a student here at Ithaca College. I **have learned so much in the academic atmosphere**, from my fellow students in the social scene, and I have grown up a lot. There are opportunities for everything that I love to do. I will never forget my experiences here and how they have helped shape me into who I am."

Q "I love IC. I can't imagine being anywhere else. **I chose IC because of the occupational therapy program.**"

Q "For the most part I like it here. The people can be really friendly and the classes are usually nice and small and not too tough. The weather tends to get people down, but I find that's true of a lot of schools. **I like the small, compact campus.** The population is the right size: small enough to say hi to plenty of friends on the way to classes, and big enough that you don't know everyone. Although transfers are somewhat common, it seems that way everywhere."

Q "I admit **the school can get boring at times because there's not a whole lot to do**, especially if you don't have a car, but the school does make an effort to provide things to do on the weekends. A lot of times with schools, people may be unhappy, but they don't feel that they'd necessarily be happier elsewhere. You could do a lot worse than Ithaca."

Q "I absolutely love Ithaca. Great experience, people are wonderful. Advice: get involved immediately in volunteer services and in activities in your major. **Get connected on campus right away** and delve into the college experience as soon as you can."

The College Prowler Take On...
Overall Experience

In evaluating their overall experience at IC, students often look to what has happened beyond the classrooms. IC offers countless opportunities to learn outside of class, and the students who take advantage of those offers are generally more pleased with their education. Many students love IC because of its size. It's hard to walk anywhere on campus without bumping into someone you know. With its great location, IC offers much off campus as well. The most common complaints are how much it costs to attend IC and the bitterly cold winter months that students have to endure.

With many things in life, students' experiences with IC are simply what they make of them. If you sit in your dorm room for four years, you will be miserable. If you experience the life Ithaca has to offer outside of the four walls of your room, you most likely won't regret your decision to attend IC. The school's high retention rate proves this. IC offers a great mix of academics and everything else the college life should offer—friends, fun, and a time to learn and grow.

The Inside Scoop

The Lowdown On...
The Inside Scoop

Ithaca Slang

Know the slang, know the school. The following is a list of things you really need to know before coming to IC. The more of these words you know, the better off you'll be.

Ball: The sculpture on top of Textor Hall. Some people say it's supposed to be a fish.

Bo-ghetto: Bogart Hall. This is one of the lower quad dormitories on campus.

Boot: Boothroyd Hall. This building has the smallest dorm rooms on campus, and is part of the First Year Program.

CSLI: Center for Student Leadership and Involvement. This office is involved with the student organizations on campus.

C-Squared: Campus Center. This is the main student center on campus.

Circles: The College Circle Apartments. These fully-furnished apartments are very popular among upperclassmen.

Gardens: Garden Apartments. Although not as new as the Circle Apartments, these are popular with students who want to live closer to campus.

Gym: The Fitness Center. Students don't say they are going to the Fitness Center to work out. They go to the gym.

H&S: The School of Humanities and Sciences.

HSHP: The School of Health Sciences and Human Performance.

LGBT: Lesbian, Gay, Bisexual, Transgender. A person is sometimes referred to as this or it is in reference to the Center for Lesbian, Gay, Bisexual, Transgender, Education, Outreach, and Services.

Parkies: Students enrolled in the Roy H. Park School of Communications.

Pub: Popular place (that doesn't actually serve alcohol) for students to study and socialize. Home to La Vincita.

Rape Road: The access road behind Rowland Hall, leading to the Towers. While rapes don't actually occur on this road, the way it's secluded makes you want to bring a friend along for the walk.

SAC: Student Activities Center. All clubs and organizations on campus have their mailboxes here, and this is where the offices for the Student Government Association are located.

SASP: Student Auxiliary Safety Patrol. Members of SASP make rounds all over campus nightly.

Suicide Bridge: The bridge at Cornell University. Sadly, some Cornell students have taken their lives on this bridge.

TCAT: Tompkins Consolidated Area Transit. Bus fare is $1.50 each way.

Quad: The area in the middle of the main campus buildings.

Z-Lot: Another name for one of the freshmen lots. Its name fits well because of its distance from most of the dorms freshmen live in.

Things I Wish I Knew Before Coming to IC

• To have a cell phone with a plan that includes free nights and weekends for those homesick times.

• Get on the smallest meal plan possible.

• Bring a car to campus if you have one and can afford the parking permit.

• Lower level classes are no indication of how much work is actually involved.

• How liberal the city of Ithaca is; no matter what your political party, Ithaca is like no other place you've been before.

• You can't get a 4.0 unless you get above a 93 percent in every class, 90-92 percent is an A- worth 3.7.

• How windy and cold it gets for half of the school year.

• Make sure to not end up living in Boothroyd.

Tips to Succeed at IC:

• Come to campus with an open mind.

• Do your reading.

• Get involved with the many organizations on campus.

• Don't be afraid to speak your mind.

• Don't be afraid to approach your professors and ask for help.

• Utilize the services the campus provides, such as the writing center and Career Services.

• Stay informed of campus happenings by reading the school paper, The Ithacan, and watching the school's television station, ICTV.

• Check your e-mail frequently.

• Ask around about your professors before you register for your classes.

• Don't take classes that, instead of listing a professor as teaching it, are listed as being taught by "staff." This is often taught by a first-semester professor, or a professor who already has a heavy class load.

IC Urban Legends:

Legend has it that a student once jumped out of the top floor of one of the towers on campus. That room supposedly has been uninhabited since, but no one can seem to find that empty room, or record of a student falling to his or her death.

Another legend remains that if your roommate dies during the year, you get an automatic 4.0—again, no such thing.

The sculpture on top of Textor Hall, which is supposedly a fish, might roll down South Hill if you're a virgin when you leave IC.

Some students claim to see the image of a swan made out of street lights when they are in the towers, and others even claim to see a certain four-letter word spelled out with the lights.

School Spirit

While everyone on campus has an IC sweatshirt, school spirit is not as prevalent here as it is at other schools. Because IC is only a Division III school in athletics, the teams tend to get overlooked. If more students paid attention to the fine talent that IC athletes have, then more students would paint their faces blue and gold and yell, "Go Bombers!"

Traditions

Convocation

During the first few days after arriving on campus and before classes start, freshmen attend the convocation ceremony where the college president and other school officials address the class. After convocation, the campus community gathers on the quad to enjoy a picnic. This is the last time the class is together as a whole until commencement.

Cortaca Jug

In November, everyone on campus gathers at the football stadium to watch the Bombers take on their rivals, the Cortland Red Dragons. This game is known as the Cortaca Jug, and Sports Illustrated calls it the "biggest little game in the nation." Some game-goers like to participate in what is known as "Kegs and Eggs" before kickoff, but being drunk is definitely not required to have a good time.

Others

Other traditions include the Ford Fest, a music extravaganza, senior week events such as Fountain Day, where all seniors jump in the fountains, and family weekend, when the families of students are invited to campus to participate in a number of different activities.

Finding a Job or Internship

The Lowdown On...
Finding a Job or Internship

As a freshman, don't expect to know exactly what you want to end up doing in four years. Many students change majors once, twice, or even three or more times. As students mature and find subject areas they have interest in, new opportunities and curiosities often arise. Throughout it all, your academic advisor and the IC Career Services will be there to assist you, and with a degree from IC, you should be on the right path to finding your dream job.

The Lowdown:

Whether during the school year or in the summertime, most students have had at least one internship before they graduate from IC. Most internships occur the summer after a students' sophomore and junior years in college. In today's highly competitive job market, most prospective employers expect to see some kind of related experience in the field that the graduate applies. The Career Services Department at IC offers many resources to find an internship.

The Lowdown (*Continued...*)
When it comes time to enter the working world, Career Services will help students with their searches. Through Network Nights and Job Fairs, many students gain valuable connections and are given the opportunity to meet potential employers.

Advice:

Students usually start trying to find an internship for the upcoming summer shortly after they arrive to school in the fall. By talking to peers who have had internships in similar fields in the past, many students find connections. Professors and IC grads can also be a valuable asset in finding internships because of their experience in specific fields. Many professional organizations that deal with students' majors operate Websites that have internship databases on them.

Don't be afraid to go to Career Services to learn more information about an internship or job. Utilize their programs, set up a mock interview, let them critique your résumé and cover letter. Money from each student's tuition goes towards Career Services, so students should take full advantage.

Career Center Resources & Services:

• On-campus job interviews

• Internships

• Resume assistance

• Alumni network

• Interest inventory

• Interview training

Alumni

The Lowdown On...
Alumni

Website:
http://www.ithaca.edu/alumni

Office:
210 Alumni Hall
Ithaca, New York 14850-7041
(607) 274-3194
alumni@ithaca.edu

Services and Benefits Available:
Online Community
Alumni Association Mastercard
Car Rental Discounts
Health and Life Insurance
Home and Auto Insurance Discounts
Hotel Discounts
Kaplan Educational Services Discounts
Legacy Admissions
Moving Services Discount
Bookstore Discounts
Career Services

➡

Major Alumni Events:
Alumni Weekend
Homecoming
Club Events
Network Nights

Alumni Publications:
Ithaca College Quarterly

Did You Know?

David Boreanaz (Class of '91), Played Angel on "Buffy the Vampire Slayer"

William D'Elia (Class of '69), Director of "The West Wing" and "American Dreams"

Arnold Gabriel (Class of '50), George Mason Symphony Conductor

Barbara Gaines (Class of '79), Producer of David Letterman Show

Robert Iger (Class of '73), Walt Disney International President

Gavin MacLeod (Class of '52), Played the captain on the show "Loveboat"

Jessica Savitch (Class of '68), Anchored the NBC Nightly News

Anthony Wise (Class of '73), Carolina Panthers Offensive Line Coach

Student Organizations

Acahtl Players

Adventure Recreation Club

African-Latino Society

Aging and Gerontologic Educational Society (AGES)

Alliance, The

Amani Gospel Singers

American Advertising Federation

American Choral Directors Association (ACDA)

American Marketing Association

American Red Cross at Ithaca College (ARC@IC)

Amnesty International

Anime Society of Ithaca College (ASIC)

Anthropology Club

Art Club

Art History Club

Asian Culture Club

ASTA (American String Teachers Association)

Awareness of Class Inequality

Balkan Express

BiGayLA

Bureau of Concerts

Buzzsaw Haircut

California Oregon Washington Association (C.O.W.ASS.)

Catholic Community Visioning Team

Chi Alpha Christian Fellowship

Chicago Club, The

Chu Jue Pool

Circle K

Colleges Against Cancer

Community Service Network (CSN)

Connectivity

Core Trading Consultants

Created Equal

Cultural Connections

Dance Collective

Dance Team

DIY Collective

East Tower Hall Association

Econutopia Club

Emerson Hall Council

Equestrian Club

Fahrenheit 451 Breakdance Club

Federation of Sport Clubs

Feminist Majority Leaders Alliance (FMLA)

Fifes and Drums of Ithaca, The

Financial Management Association

French Circle

Friends of Israel

Hall Council HHHE

Health Policy and Management Association (HPMA)

Health Promotion and Human Movement (HPHM) Majors Club

Hillel

IC Athletic Training Students' Association

IC Comedy Club

IC Democrats

IC Filmmakers Association

IC for Dean

IC Guiding Eyes

IC Guitar Club

IC Hip Hop Dance

IC Jazz Club

IC Men's Club Soccer

IC PEACE

IC Players

IC Spanish Club

IC Steel Band Club

IC Tap Dance Club

IC Unbound Dance Company

Interfraternity Council

International Business Association

International Club

Ithaca Band Organization

Ithaca College Accounting Association

Ithaca College Carribean Students Association

Ithaca College Cheerleading Team

Ithaca College Chemistry Society

Ithaca College Djembe Ensemble

Ithaca College Documentary Society

Ithaca College Enchre

Ithaca College Environmental Society

Ithaca College Habitat for Humanity

Ithaca College Heifer International (ICHI)

Ithaca College Men's Club Lacrosse

Ithaca College Men's Ice Hockey

Ithaca College Philosophy Club

Ithaca College Republicans

Ithaca College Student Occupational Therapy Association (ICSOTA)

Ithaca College Tae Kwon Do Club

Ithaca College Triple Threat Theatre

Ithaca College Trombone Troupe

Ithaca College Writing Workshop (ICW2)

Ithacappella (Ithaca College Men's Chorus)

Ivory Tower Gaming Society

Justice and Peace Chapter - Catholic Community

Kappa Gamma Psi

Knitting Circle, The

KUUMBA

Lambda Pi Eta

Lamda Pi Eta

Landon-Bogart-Lyon-Clarke Hall Council

Men's Volleyball

Minority Business Student's Association

Mu Phi Epsilon

Music Educators National Conference (MENC)

National Broadcasting Society (NBS)

National Student Speech-Language-Hearing Association (NSSHLA)

Native American Cultural Club

Organizational Communication, Learning and Design Assocation

(OCLDA)

Orgullo Latino

Other Realms

Phi Mu Alpha Sinfonia

Pi Mu Epsilon/Math Club

Pi Theta Epsilon

Ping Pong

Pre-Medical Society

Premium Blend

Professional Wrestling Fan Club

Protestant Community at Ithaca College

Public Relations Student Society of America (PRSSA)

REACH

Residence Hall Association (RHA)

Rotaract Club

Seido Karate

Senior Class

Sigma Alpha Iota

Sigma Iota Epsilon

Sigma Phi Omega

Ski Team/Club

Social Enrichment for All

Social Studies Education Club

Society of Professional Journalists

Sport Management Activities Club

Sport Psychology Students' Association

Student Activities Board

Student Alumni Association

Student Athletic Advisory Council

Student Government Association

Student Psychology Association

Student Sociology Association

Students Against Destructive Decisions (SADD)

Students for a Just Peace

Students for Christ

Students for Economic Awareness

Students for Life

Students in Free Enterprise

Sword Team of Ithaca

Sword Team of Ithaca College

Terraces 9-12 Hall Council

Topalov

Ultimate Frisbee Club

UNICEF

United Way of Ithaca College

Voice Stream

Women's Club Lacrosse

Women's Club Soccer

Women's Club Volleyball

Women's Rugby

The Best &
The Worst

The Ten **BEST** Things About IC:

1	The friendly people
2	Many extracurricular activities
3	Cortaca Jug
4	The facilities (Fitness Center, Park, science buildings, residence halls)
5	Living in a college town
6	The view from campus
7	Surrounding outdoor activities
8	Great local restaurants
9	Safety on campus
10	The occasional beautiful weather

The Ten **WORST** Things About IC:

1 The winter weather

2 Since IC is on a hill, climbing all the stairs

3 The price

4 Many professors are hit or miss

5 Not many big name performers or comedians come to campus

6 Not enough school spirit

7 Administrators don't communicate enough with students

8 Too much red tape everywhere

9 Unreliable computer network

10 No Greek life

Visiting IC

The Lowdown On...
Visiting IC

Hotel Information

Ithaca:

Best Western University Inn
http://www.bestwestern.com
1020 Ellis Hollow Road
Ithaca, NY 14850
(607) 272-6100 or 1-800-528-1234
Price Range: $89-$209

Clarion University Hotel & Conference Center
http://www.choicehotels.com
One Sheraton Drive
Ithaca, NY 14850
(607) 257-2000
Price Range: $69-$250

Comfort Inn
http://www.comfortinn.com/ny199
356 Elmira Road
Ithaca, NY 14850
(607) 272-0100 or 1-800-228-5150
Price Range: $65-$155

Econo Lodge
http://www.econolodge.com/hotel/ny127
2303 N. Triphammer Road
Ithaca, NY 14850
(607) 257-1400
Price Range: $46-$115

→

Economy Inn
http://www.economyinnithaca.com
658 Elmira Road
Ithaca, NY 14850
(607) 277-0370
Price Range: $36-$115

Embassy Inn
1083 Dryden Road
Ithaca, NY 14850
(607) 272-3721
Price Range: $45-$85

Grayhaven Motel
http://www.grayhavenmotel.com
657 Elmira Road
Ithaca, NY 14850
(607) 272-6434 or 1-877-241-6434
Price Range: $50-125

Hillside Inn
http://www.hillside-inn.net
518 Stewart Ave.
Ithaca, NY 14850
(607) 272-9507
Price Range: $30-$85

Holiday Inn- Executive Tower
http://www.holidayinnithaca.com
222 S. Cayuga St.
Ithaca, NY 14850
(607) 272-1000 or 1-800-753-8485
Price Range: $69-$199

Ithaca Courtyard Marriot
http://www.courtyard.com
29 Thornwood Drive
Ithaca, NY 14850
(607) 330-1000 or 1-800-321-2211
Price Range: $109-$169

La Tourelle Country Inn
http://www.latourelleinn.com
1150 Danby Road
Ithaca, NY 14850
(607) 273-2734 or 1-800-765-1492
Price Range: $89-$250

Meadow Court Inn
529 S. Meadow St.
Ithaca, NY 14850
(607) 273-3885 or 1-800-852-4014
Price Range: $45-$295

Ramada Inn- Training & Conference Center
http://www.ramada.com
2310 N. Triphammer Road
Ithaca, NY 14850
(607) 257-3100
Price Range: $69-$250

The Rose Inn
http://www.roseinn.com
Route 34N, Box 6576
Ithaca, NY 14850
(607) 533-7905
Price Range: $155-$325

The Statler Hotel
http://www.statlerhotel.cornell.edu
East Ave. at Cornell University
Ithaca, NY 14853
(607) 257-2500 or 1-800-541-2501
Price Range: $105-$300

Super 8 Motel
http://www.super8.com
400 S. Meadow St.
Ithaca, NY 14850
(607) 273-8088 or 1-800-800-8000
Price Range: $50-$115

Wonderland Inn & Suites
http://www.wonderlandmotel.com
654 Elmira Road
Ithaca, NY 14850
(607) 272-5252
Price Range: $45-$95

Take a Campus Virtual Tour

http://www.ithaca.edu/tour/

To Schedule a Group Information Session or Interview:

The admissions staff encourages students to set up an interview at least two weeks in advance. Call (800) 429-4274.

Campus Tours:

Campus tours are held hourly from 9 a.m.-3 p.m. weekdays, and from 9 a.m.-11 a.m. on most Saturdays when college is in session. Tours are also available during the summer on Saturdays in July and August. It is encouraged to call the admissions office at (800) 429-4274 at least two weeks in advance to schedule an appointment.

Overnight Visits:

Prospective students are encouraged to spend a night on campus to get a real look at college life. Students will get a taste of classes and what residential life is really like. Call the admissions office at (800) 429-4274 or (607) 274-3124 at least two weeks in advance to schedule your stay.

Other Visit Opportunities:

Ithaca and you! Programs are offered throughout the academic year and include special group sessions, academic presentations, and tours.

Open houses are held on select Saturdays in the fall and include tours of the campus and more in-depth academic sessions.

For accepted students and their families, Ithaca Today is a special in the Schools of Business, Communications, Humanities and Sciences, and Health Sciences and Human Performance to involve the students in their school for a day.

For more information, prospective students should call the admissions office at (800) 429-4274 or visit www.ithaca.edu/admissions.

Overnight Visits:

Driving from the New York City Area:

• Follow Route 17 (soon to be I-86) west to Binghamton.

• Take I-81 north to exit 8 at Whitney Point.

• Follow Route 79 west into Ithaca.

• At T-intersection turn left onto Route 96B (Aurora St.) and follow 96B south for approximately one mile. The campus will be on your left.

Driving from Albany and New England:

• Follow the New York State Thruway (I-90) west to I-88 (exit 25A).

• Take I-88 west to Bainbridge (exit 8) and then Route 206 to Whitney Point.

• Pick up Route 79 west to Ithaca.

• At T-intersection turn left onto Route 96B (Aurora St.) and follow 96B south for approximately one mile. The campus will be on your left.

Driving from Rochester and Buffalo:

• Follow the New York State Thruway (I-90) east to exit 41 at Waterloo. Do not follow the signs that direct you to Ithaca via Geneva.

• Turn right after the toll booth onto Route 414 south.

• Turn left at the red light onto Route 318 east.

• Follow Route 318 east several miles.

• At the T-intersection turn left, then a quick right onto Route 89 to Ithaca.

• Pick up Route 13 South in Ithaca.

• After passing Green St., move into the far left lane and go straight onto Route 96B (Clinton St.)

• Turn right onto Aurora St. (still 96B) and continue for approximately one mile. The campus will be on your left.

Driving from the Eastern Pennsylvania and points south:

• Take I-81 north to Whitney Point (exit 8).

• Pick up Route 79 west to Ithaca.

• At T-intersection turn left onto Route 96B (Aurora St.) and follow 96B south for approximately one mile. The campus will be on your left.

Driving from the Erie, Pennsylvania and points west:

• Follow Route 17 (soon to be I-86) east to exit 54 and take Route 13 north into Ithaca.

• Turn right onto Route 96B (Clinton St.) and continue to Aurora St.

• Turn right onto Aurora St. (still 96B) and continue for approximately one mile. The campus will be on your left.

Driving from the Syracuse and points north:

• Follow I-81 south to Cortland (exit 12).

• Take Route 281 south to Route 13 south to Ithaca.

• After passing Green St., move into the far left lane and go straight onto Route 96B (Clinton St.)

Turn right onto Aurora St. (still 96B) and continue for approximately one mile. The campus will be on your left.

Words to Know

Academic Probation – A student can receive this if they fail to keep up with their school's academic minimums. Those who are unable to improve their grades after receiving this warning can possibly face dismissal.

Beer Pong / Beirut – A drinking game with numerous cups of beer arranged in a particular pattern on each side of a table. The goal is to get a ping pong ball into one of the opponent's cups by throwing the ball or hitting it with a paddle. If the ball lands in a cup, the opponent is required to drink the beer.

Bid – An invitation from a fraternity or sorority to pledge their specific house.

Blue-Light Phone – Brightly-colored phone posts with a blue light bulb on top. These phones exist for security purposes and are located at various outside locations around most campuses. If a student has an emergency or is feeling endangered, they can pick up one of these phones (free of charge) to connect with campus police or an escort service.

Campus Police – Policemen who are specifically assigned to a given institution. Campus police are not regular city officers; they are employed by the university in a full-time capacity.

Club Sports – A level of sports that falls somewhere between varsity and intramural. If a student is unable to commit to a varsity team but has a lot of passion for athletics, a club sport could be a better, less intense option. If a club sport still requires too much commitment, intramurals often involve no traveling and a lot less time.

Cocaine – An illegal drug. Also known as "coke" or "blow," cocaine often resembles a white crystalline or powdery substance. It is highly addictive and dangerous.

Common Application – An application that students can use to apply to multiple schools.

Course Registration – The time when a student selects what courses they would like for the upcoming quarter or semester. Prior to registration, it is best to have an idea of several back-up courses in case a particular class becomes full. If a course is full, a student can place themselves on the waitlist, although this still does not guarantee entry.

Division Athletics – Athletics range from Division I to Division III. Division IA is the most competitive, while Division III is considered to be the least competitive.

Dorm – Short for dormitory, a dorm is an on-campus housing facility. Dorms can provide a range of options from suite-style rooms to more communal options that include shared bathrooms. Most first-year students live in dorms. Some upperclassmen who wish to stay on campus also choose this option.

Early Action – A way to apply to a school and get an early acceptance response without a binding commitment. This is a system that is becoming less and less available.

Early Decision – An option that students should use only if they are positive that a place is their dream school. If a student applies to a school using the early decision option and is admitted, they are required and bound to attend that university. Admission rates are usually higher with early decision students because the school knows that a student is making them their first choice.

Ecstasy – An illegal drug. Also known as "E" or "X," ecstasy looks like a pill and most resembles an aspirin. Considered a party drug, ecstasy is very dangerous and can be deadly.

Ethernet – An extremely fast internet connection that is usually available in most university-owned residence halls. To use an Ethernet connection properly, a student will need a network card and cable for their computer.

Fake ID – A counterfeit identification card that contains false information. Most commonly, students get fake IDs and change their birthdates so that they appear to be older than 21 (of legal drinking age). Even though it is illegal, many college students have fake IDs in hopes of purchasing alcohol or getting into bars.

Frosh – Slang for "freshmen."

Hazing – Initiation rituals that must be completed for membership into some fraternities or sororities. Numerous universities have outlawed hazing due to its degrading or dangerous requirements.

Sports (IMs) – A popular, and usually free, student activity where students create teams and compete against other groups for fun. These sports vary in competitiveness and can include a range of activities—everything from billiards to water polo. IM sports are a great way to meet people with similar interests.

Keg – Officially called a half barrel, a keg contains roughly 200 12-ounce servings of beer and is often found at college parties.

LSD – An illegal drug. Also known as acid, this hallucinogenic drug most commonly resembles a tab of paper.

Marijuana – An illegal drug. Also known as weed or pot; besides alcohol, marijuana is one of the most commonly-found drugs on campuses across the country.

Major –The focal point of a student's college studies; a specific topic that is studied for a degree. Examples of majors include physics, English, history, computer science, economics, business, and music. Many students decide on a specific major before arriving on campus, while others are simply "undecided" and figure it out later. Those who are extremely interested in two areas can also choose to double major.

Meal Block – The equivalent of one meal. Students on a "meal plan" usually receive a fixed number of meals per week.

Each meal, or "block," can be redeemed at the school's dining facilities in place of cash. More often than not, if a student fails to use their weekly allotment of meal blocks, they will be forfeited.

Minor – An additional focal point in a student's education. Often serving as a compliment or addition to a student's main area of focus, a minor has fewer requirements and prerequisites to fulfill than a major. Minors are not required for graduation from most schools; however some students who want to further explore many different interests choose to have both a major and a minor.

Mushrooms – An illegal drug. Also known as "shrooms," this drug looks like regular mushrooms but are extremely hallucinogenic.

Off-Campus Housing – Housing from a particular landlord or rental group that is not affiliated with the university. Depending on the college, off-campus housing can range from extremely popular to non-existent. Those students who choose to live off campus are typically given more freedom, but they also have to deal with things such as possible subletting scenarios, furniture, and bills. In addition to these factors, rental prices and distance often affect a student's decision to move off campus.

Office Hours – Time that teachers set aside for students who have questions about the coursework. Office hours are a good place for students to go over any problems and to show interest in the subject material.

Pledging – The time after a student has gone through rush, received a bid, and has chosen a particular fraternity or sorority they would like to join. Pledging usually lasts anywhere from one to two semesters. Once the pledging period is complete and a particular student has done everything that is required to become a member, they are considered a brother or sister. If a fraternity or a sorority would decide to "haze" a group of students, these initiation rituals would take place during the pledging period.

Private Institution – A school that does not use taxpayers dollars to help subsidize education costs. Private schools typically cost more than public schools and are usually smaller.

Prof – Slang for "professor."

Public Institution – A school that uses taxpayers dollars to help subsidize education costs. Public schools are often a good value for in-state residents and tend to be larger than most private colleges.

Quarter System (sometimes referred to as the Trimester System) – A type of academic calendar system. In this setup, students take classes for three academic periods. The first quarter usually starts in late September or early October and concludes right before Christmas. The second quarter usually starts around early to mid–January and finishes up around March or April. The last quarter, or "third quarter," usually starts in late March or early April and finishes up in late May or Mid-June. The fourth quarter is summer. The major difference between the quarter system and semester system is that students take more courses but with less coverage.

RA (Resident Assistant) – A student leader who is assigned to a particular floor in a dormitory in order to help to the other students who live there. A RA's duties include ensuring student safety and providing guidance or assistance wherever possible.

Recitation – An extension of a specific course; a "review" session of sorts. Because some classes are so large, recitations offer a setting with fewer students where students can ask questions and get help from professors or TAs in a more personalized environment. As a result, it is common for most large lecture classes to be supplemented with recitations.

Rolling Admissions – A form of admissions. Most commonly found at public institutions, schools with this type of policy continue to accept students throughout the year until their class sizes are met. For example, some schools begin accepting students as early as December and will continue to do so until April or May.

Room and Board – This is typically the combined cost of a university-owned room and a meal plan.

Room Draw/Housing Lottery – A common way to pick on-campus room assignments for the following year. If a student decides to remain in university-owned housing, they are assigned a unique number that, along with seniority, is used to choose their new rooms for the next year.

Rush – The period in which students can meet the brothers and sisters of a particular chapter and find out if a given fraternity or sorority is right for them. Rushing a fraternity or a sorority is not a requirement at any school. The goal of rush is to give students who are serious about pledging a feel for what to expect.

Semester System – The most common type of academic calendar system at college campuses. This setup typically includes two semesters in a given school year. The "fall" semester starts around the end of August or early September and finishes right before winter vacation. The "spring" semester usually starts in mid-January and ends around late April or May.

Student Center/Rec Center/Student Union – A common area on campus that often contains study areas, recreation facilities, and eateries. This building is often a good place to meet up with fellow students and is most commonly used as a hangout. Depending on the school, the student center can have a huge role or a non-existent role in campus life.

Student ID – A university-issued photo ID that serves as a student's key to many different functions within an institution. Some schools require students to show these cards in order to get into dorms, libraries, cafeterias, and other facilities. In addition to storing meal plan information, in some cases, a student ID can actually work as a debit card and allow students to purchase things from bookstores or local shops.

Suite – A type of dorm room. Unlike other places that have communal bathrooms that are shared by the entire floor, a suite has a private bathroom. Suite-style dorm rooms can house anywhere from two to ten students.

TA (Teacher's Assistant) – An undergraduate or grad student who helps in some manner with a specific course. In some cases, a TA will teach a class, assist a professor, grade assignments, or conduct office hours.

Undergraduate – A student who is in the process of studying for their Bachelor (college) degree.

ABOUT THE AUTHOR:

As a reporter for the college newspaper, The Ithacan, I considered myself very knowledgeable about IC before I wrote this book. Now, as I have visited practically every Ithaca website and every department at IC, I know more than I ever wanted to know! But seriously, I really enjoyed getting the chance to write this book, and I hope that it has helped you in your decision about IC.

My experience thus far at IC hasn't been anything short of amazing. Just a sophomore, I feel that I've accomplished so much inside and outside of the classroom, met so many interesting people, and know so much more about myself than I ever thought I would by now. As a journalism major from Erie, Pennsylvania, my love for the skill of reporting and writing has grown even stronger with my work with The Ithacan, the IC yearbook, The Cayugan, and this guide to IC, the first book by myself.

Without these people's help and encouragement, I would never have completed this book: my family, Chris, my apartment-mates Anne, Liz, and Michelle, my wonderful Parkie friends, the staff at various offices on campus who put up with my persistency, and everyone at College Prowler. Thank You!

Sarah Hofius

Notes

....

....

....

....

....

....

....

....

....

....

....

....

....

Do You Have What It Takes To Get Admitted?

The College Prowler Road to College Counseling Program is here. An admissions officer will review your candidacy at the school of your choice and create a 12+ page personal admission plan. We rate your credentials with the same criteria used by school admissions committees. We assess your strengths and weaknesses and create a plan of action that makes a difference.

Check out **www.collegeprowler.com** or call 1.800.290.2682 for complete details.

Notes

....

....

....

....

....

....

....

....

....

....

....

....

....

Pros and Cons

Still can't figure out if this is the right school for you?
You've already read through this in-depth guide; why not
list the pros and cons? It will really help with narrowing down
your decision and determining whether or not
this school is right for you.

Pros	Cons

Notes

....

....

....

....

....

....

....

....

....

....

....

....

....

Need Help Paying For School?
Apply for our Scholarship!

College Prowler awards thousands of dollars a year
to students who compose the best essays.
E-mail *scholarship@collegeprowler.com* for more
information, or call 1.800.290.2682.

Apply now at **www.collegeprowler.com**

Notes

....

....

....

....

....

....

....

....

....

....

....

....

....

Notes

....

....

....

....

....

....

....

....

....

....

....

....

....

Notes

....

....

....

....

....

....

....

....

....

....

....

....

....

....

Notes

....

....

....

....

....

....

....

....

....

....

....

....

....

....

Write For Us!

Get Published! Voice Your Opinion.

Writing a College Prowler guidebook is both fun and rewarding; our open-ended format allows your own creativity free reign. Our writers have been featured in national newspapers and have seen their names in bookstores across the country. Now is your chance to break into the publishing industry with one of the country's fastest-growing publishers!

Apply now at **www.collegeprowler.com**

Contact *editor@collegeprowler.com* or call 1.800.290.2682 for more details.

Tell Us What Life Is Really Like At Your School!

Have you ever wanted to let people know what your school is really like? Now's your chance to help millions of high school students choose the right school.

Let your voice be heard and win cash and prizes!

Check out **www.collegeprowler.com** for more info!